HISTORY IN THE MAKING

OTT

HISTORY
IN THE
MAKING

YALE UNIVERSITY PRESS
NEW HAVEN AND LONDON

For information about this and other Yale University Press publications, please contact:
U.S. Office: sales.press@yale.edu www.yalebooks.com
Europe Office: sales @yaleup.co.uk www.yalebooks.co.uk

Set in Adobe Caslon by IDSUK (DataConnection) Ltd
Printed in Great Britain by TJ International Ltd, Padstow, Cornwall

Library of Congress Cataloging-in-Publication Data

Elliott, John Huxtable.
    History in the making / John H. Elliott.
        p. cm.
    ISBN 978-0-300-18638-3 (cl : alk. paper)
1. Spain—Historiography.   2. Historiography.   3. Elliott, John
Huxtable.   I. Title.
    DP63.E35 2012
    946.0072'02—dc23

                                                            2012017210

A catalogue record for this book is available from the British Library.

10 9 8 7 6 5 4 3 2 1

For Oonah
who has lived with the consequences

Contents

Illustrations

1 Diego de Velázquez, *The Count-Duke of Olivares on Horseback* (*c.* 1638). Museo del Prado, Madrid.

2 The castle archive of Simancas.

3 The author with the Coderch family (1954). Author's photograph.

4 Jaume Vicens Vives and Ferran Soldevila (1957). By permission of the heirs of Jaume Vicens Vives and Editorial Vicens Vives.

5 Stephen Farthing, *Historians of 'Past and Present'* (1999). © National Portrait Gallery, London.

6 Diego de Velázquez, *The Surrender of Breda* (1634–5). Museo del Prado, Madrid.

7 Attributed to Jusepe Leonardo, *Palace of the Buen Retiro* (1636–7). Patrimonio Nacional.

8 The author and Jonathan Brown (2005). Photograph by Ricardo Gutiérrez, *El País*.

9 Hernán Cortés, *John Elliott* (2001–2).

Preface

THIS is both an impersonal and a personal book. It is impersonal in that it explores some of the themes and problems addressed by historians during the second half of the twentieth century and the opening years of the twenty-first. It is personal because the period since the 1950s is the one which covers my own career as a practising historian. It therefore expresses, in the light of my personal experiences, views on the practice of history as it has developed over the course of my professional life. It is personal, too, in that I have selected various of my own publications as launching-pads for the discussion of topics which, although of particular interest to me, would seem to raise issues of interest to anyone who enjoys reading and writing about the past. It is, however, in no sense intended as an *apologia pro vita sua*, although it may sometimes read as such. Dr George Kitson Clark, the historian of nineteenth-century Britain who was my mentor during my days as an undergraduate at Trinity College, Cambridge, used to recite from Kipling,

> There are nine and sixty ways of constructing tribal lays,
> And every single one of them is right![1]

While I do not think that this is wholly true where the writing of history is concerned, it implies an attitude of tolerance towards different approaches to the depiction of the past that I have tried to make my own.

Rather than laying down guidelines, therefore, the book attempts to explore some of the issues that have faced historians in general, and this historian in particular, over the past five or six decades as they have tried to make sense of the past. These have been decades of immense change, both in approaches to the past and in the character of the historical profession itself. The proliferation of universities and history departments in the western world has led to an enormous increase in the number of academic historians. Large numbers of women have entered a profession which, before the middle decades of the twentieth century, was almost exclusively dominated by men. At the same time, traditional disciplinary boundaries have been eroded with the result that the past has become an open terrain over which representatives of all the humanist disciplines have felt free to roam at will. While all this has led to a vast enrichment of our understanding of history and of the historical process itself, it has also led to extensive and often polemical debate about what we can actually know, and recover, of the past, and indeed whether there is any objective past waiting to be recovered.

I must confess to never having been particularly interested in this debate, nor indeed in theoretical approaches to the study of the past. British historians are often reproached for being excessively pragmatic, but over the last half-century, without beating theoretical drums, they have set high standards in exploring and writing about the past, not only of their own country but also of that of foreign nations and societies. I believe that theory is of less importance for the writing of good history than the ability to enter imaginatively into the life of a society remote in time or place, and produce a plausible explanation of why its inhabitants thought and behaved as they did.

The bulk of my own research and writing was done before the advent of computerization in a readily accessible form. This book, coming at it does from a representative of the last generation of pre-digital historians, may therefore in itself be of some historical interest, if only as a record. Future generations, no longer constrained by limited opening hours and uncertain working conditions in libraries and archives, may well look back in mingled astonishment and incomprehension at the activities of their predecessors, armed with little more than pen and notebook, and wonder at the vast gaps in the information at their command.

Yet, for all the increase in information that can be expected from the deployment of the electronic resources now available to historians, the problems they have always faced will continue to confront them. The attempt to pin down the past is an elusive enterprise, and every serious historian is painfully aware of the gulf that exists between the aspiration and its realization. Yet the attempt to bridge this gulf is as exciting as it is frustrating. The excitement comes from the challenge of attempting to break loose from contemporary attitudes and assumptions, while simultaneously recognizing the constraints they impose. The sensation, after immersing oneself in an earlier age, of being within touching distance of its inhabitants and at least acquiring a partial understanding of their behaviour and intentions, is a powerful one, and makes historical research an immensely rewarding experience. I hope in the course of this book to suggest the kind of rewards that the study of the past has to offer, and convey something of the enjoyment that the writing of history can bring.

Acknowledgements

WHEN I first, very tentatively, suggested to Robert Baldock that Yale University Press, my publisher for more than thirty years, might be interested in a book of personal reflections on my career as a historian and on changes and developments in the writing of history over the course of my working life, he warmly welcomed the proposal. Since then he has been an ideal editor, encouraging and cajoling his author at moments when the going was rough, commenting on each chapter as it appeared, and watching with eagle eye over each stage of the book's development as it moved towards publication. I am very grateful to him, as also to his dedicated team: Candida Brazil, Tami Halliday, and Stephen Kent, whose work on the illustrations includes the striking design of the cover. I am also grateful to Laura Davey for her expert copy-editing, Lucy Isenberg for proofreading and to Meg Davies for the preparation of the index.

I am indebted, too, to my friend and former co-author, Jonathan Brown of the Institute of Fine Arts, New York University, and to my one-time research assistant in Princeton, Xavier Gil, now a professor of history in the University of Barcelona, for their valuable comments on the chapters I asked them to read. Quentin Skinner most generously offered to read the entire text, and I am deeply grateful to him both for his encouraging response and for his characteristically acute observations, which I have borne in mind in the final stages of revision.

The book is dedicated to my wife, in profound gratitude for her companionship and unswerving support during the more than fifty years of history in the making.

Oriel College, Oxford
19 April 2012

CHAPTER ONE

Why Spain?

I BECAME a historian of Spain largely by accident. In the summer of 1950, near the end of my first year reading history at Cambridge University, I saw a notice in *Varsity*, the undergraduate newspaper, saying that a few places remained for an expedition round the Iberian peninsula in an old army truck. With no plans in mind for the summer vacation I decided to sign on, and for six weeks in the heat of July and August we drove round Spain and Portugal, staying in cheap boarding houses or spending the night camping out in olive groves, sometimes to find ourselves woken at dawn by an annoyed peasant farmer who told us to clear off from his land.

Those six weeks represented my first exposure to Spain, and they made a deep impression. The country, only just beginning to take the first steps on the road to recovery in the aftermath of the Civil War, was miserably poor, and, especially in

Andalusia, children would cluster round begging for food or coins as we emerged from our truck, or sat drinking coffee in the town square. Yet, amidst all the misery and the poverty there was also enormous dignity – the dignity of a proud people who were passing through hard times but knew their own worth. I was impressed, too, by the countryside, the open expanses of the great central plain of Castile, lying parched and yellow beneath the burning summer sun. The richness and beauty of monumental Spain, the cathedrals, churches and historic centres of the cities of the interior, like Toledo, Salamanca, Ávila and Segovia, fascinated me, and I was over-whelmed by the paintings in the Prado, and especially by those of Velázquez, whose work I barely knew.

Not surprisingly, I returned to Cambridge an enthusiast for the country, although at that stage with no thought of becoming a professional historian. I was still getting to grips with the history syllabus at Cambridge, tackling subjects that were quite new to me. At school, at Eton, to which I had won a scholarship, I switched as soon as I could from the classics to modern languages, where I specialized in French and German. But I had always had a taste for history and, in my early years as a schoolboy at the preparatory school of which my father was headmaster, would devour historical novels in the well-stocked school library, and pore over the text and illustrations of the capacious volumes, bound in green, of *The Romance of the Nation: A Stirring Pageant of the British Peoples through the Ages*, published in the mid-1930s. In deciding to read for the historical rather than the modern languages Tripos at

Cambridge I was therefore returning to an early enthusiasm, although I was also motivated by the feeling that I now had sufficient knowledge of the two languages to continue reading the classics of French and German literature on my own.

The historical Tripos represented both a novelty and something of a challenge. The course at that time was very broad-based, covering as it did English constitutional and economic history, and general medieval and modern European history, together with the history of political thought. There was therefore a great deal of ground to cover, and for much of my first year I was struggling. But reading brought enjoyment, and enjoyment brought a growing sense of mastery. I was stimulated by some of the college teaching I received, not least in medieval history, where the contrasting approaches of my two tutors left me with an almost schizophrenic view of the Middle Ages: Walter Ullmann, the obsessive historian of canon law and the medieval papacy, fiercely inquisitorial in his tutorials, although often with a twinkle in his eye, and Steven Runciman, deceptively languid in manner, who would introduce me to what seemed highly esoteric topics drawn from the history of societies on the fringes of medieval Europe. I learned a great deal, too, from some of the university lecturers whose courses I attended: J. H. Plumb, delivering his exhilarating lectures on eighteenth-century England with machine-gun rapidity; Herbert Butterfield, piling up the complexities as he grappled with the enigmas of modern European history; and Dom David Knowles, gently but firmly guiding us through the intricacies of medieval philosophical argument. By the end of my third year I had decided that, if the opportunity arose, I would like to devote the next few years to historical research. My college, Trinity, was sympathetic and my tutors encouraging, and the way was open for me to embark on the life of a research student.

Temperament, upbringing, chance and calculation – all come into play, although in varying combinations and to varying degrees, in determining why and how historians choose their subject. For a moment I toyed with the thought of research into eighteenth-century English political history, which I had found attractive as an undergraduate. But once again I felt the lure of Spain, and second thoughts prevailed. I had some talent for foreign languages; a foreign topic seemed to offer more exciting opportunities, both for travel and for discovery, than a subject chosen from the history of my own country; and already, in the early 1950s, it was borne in on me that, if I wanted to have an academic career, there was standing-room only in British history. During the summer vacation after graduating I went to Santiago de Compostela to take a summer course in Spanish, and although the course itself taught me little, the time spent in this most beautiful of cities confirmed me in my belief that studying the history of Spain and Spanish civilization was what appealed most of all.

Back in Cambridge I went to consult Herbert Butterfield, the Professor of Modern History, and told him of my interest. His response was enthusiastic, and he was encouraging about the need in British universities for a better knowledge and understanding of the history of Spain. Although Spanish literature was well represented in university departments of Romance languages, there were very few historians of Spain in the country, and least of all historians with a specialist interest in its seventeenth century, the period to which I felt most drawn. This may partly have been a consequence of the Spanish Civil War and its impact on the generation before my own. Many members of that generation, who had watched the Spanish Republic go down in defeat, refused to visit Spain as long as General Franco remained in power. I was too young to have any clear memories of the Civil War, and although strongly opposed to the regime, did not feel that my hostility to it should deter me from seeking to know better the country and its history. Somehow Spain drew me more than France and Italy, both of which I had visited in my undergraduate years. Spain, or so it seemed to me, was 'different', as claimed by Spain's ministry of tourism in the 1960s, with a slogan that would promptly be taken up and used for their own purposes both by supporters and by opponents of the Franco regime.

That sense of difference had been felt by generations of British travellers and scholars. British Hispanism has a long and distinguished history, going back at least to the eighteenth century, when Robert Watson published his histories of the reigns of Philip II and Philip III, and William Robertson, a far better historian than Watson, won international acclaim for his *History of the Reign of the Emperor Charles V*, and then for his *History of America*. The appeal of Spain, which was felt in the nineteenth century by many artists, writers and scholars, including the historian and art historian William Stirling Maxwell and the incomparable Richard Ford, the author of the *Handbook for Travellers in Spain* (1845), may in part represent the attraction of opposites. In embarking on research into Spanish history, I would be just one more in a long line of curious Protestant northerners driven by some inner compulsion to explore the alien world of the Iberian peninsula.[1]

By the time of my visit to Herbert Butterfield, who agreed to accept me as his research student, I had some idea not only of the area but also of the subject on which I wanted to work. Among the paintings by Velázquez that attracted me on the two or three visits I had by now paid to the Prado, one in particular stood out. This was his great equestrian portrait of the Count-Duke – the Conde-Duque – of Olivares, the favourite and principal minister of Philip IV from 1621 to 1643 (Plate 1). There he sits on his rearing bay horse, a massive, rather hunched figure in black and gold armour with silver highlights, and wearing the red sash of a captain-general. He points with his baton towards a distant battlefield, but it is above all the face that commands attention. In three-quarter profile, displaying his tufted beard and upturned mustachios, he looks imperiously back to the left, as if to make sure that the ranks behind him stand ready to follow him into battle. No matter that in reality he never commanded his troops on this or any other battlefield. If ever there was a portrait that embodied the arrogance of power, this must surely be it.

The painting lodged in my mind, and left me curious to find out more about the man and his times. The early seventeenth century was the Golden Age – the *siglo de oro* – of

Spanish art and literature. It was also the period in which Spain, the dominant power in Europe since the middle years of the sixteenth century, appeared to be manifesting the first symptoms of decline – a decline that would become pronounced from the 1640s onwards, when it would lose its European hegemony to the France of Louis XIV and become a society characterized in the eyes of contemporaries by economic and technological backwardness, religious obscurantism and a general torpor that left it lagging far behind its European rivals. A study built around the ministry of Olivares, as the man who governed Spain during those critical two decades, the 1620s and 1630s, when the country stood on the cusp between grandeur and decadence, might perhaps provide some clues to what had traditionally been seen as a historical conundrum, the 'decline of Spain'.

The field, moreover, seemed wide open. While Olivares made brief appearances in standard works on seventeenth-century Europe and the Thirty Years War, he received little space in comparison with that accorded to his great and ultimately victorious rival, Cardinal Richelieu. During my summer course in Santiago de Compostela I had come across an abbreviated version of what turned out to be the only modern biography of the Count-Duke, published in 1936, that most unhappy of years for modern Spain. This had been written not by a professional historian but by the eminent Spanish physician Gregorio Marañón (1887–1960), who would go on to produce other important historical works during the course of a distinguished career.[2] As I made my way, with my still uncertain Spanish, through Marañón's book, I soon saw that, while this was a highly interesting biography and a fascinating early example of psychohistory, the author was more interested in unravelling the strands of his subject's complex personality than in examining in any great detail the trajectory of his political career and the nature of his government.

As I explored further, I found that, outside the realm of art and literature, seventeenth-century Spain had not fared well at the hands of its historians. The most serious work done on the Olivares period had been produced by Antonio Cánovas del Castillo (1828–97), the nineteenth-century statesman whose historical interests inevitably took second place to his political career. Since Cánovas, not much significant archival work had been done on the period, although the topic of Spain's 'decline' remained a subject of continuing, and often agonized, debate. In general, Spain's historians had preferred to devote their attention to the great age of imperial Spain, the reigns of Ferdinand and Isabella, Charles V and Philip II, rather than get to grips with the more melancholy reigns of their lesser Habsburg descendants, Philip III and IV, and Carlos II, the last monarch of the House of Austria, whose miserable life and lingering death seemed to encapsulate the end of Spanish greatness.

Seventeenth-century Spain, then, seemed to offer ample opportunities for pioneering research, but it was far from clear what direction it should take. I was not tempted by a biographical approach, which anyhow appeared inappropriate for a doctoral dissertation. I was particularly interested in questions of government and policy-making, but my reading of

Fernand Braudel's great work *La Méditerranée et le monde méditerranéen à l'époque de Philippe II,* which had been published in the year I went up to Cambridge, 1949, had made a deep impression on me. It made me aware, in particular, that political and diplomatic history were only part of the story, and I responded strongly to Braudel's appeal to historians to commit themselves to the writing of 'total history'. This was the period when Marxist and *marxisant* history, particularly of the kind practised by the *Annales* school in Paris, of which Braudel and Lucien Febvre were the leading proponents, was sweeping everything before it. While strongly resisting a determinist approach, I was, however, convinced of the need to pay due attention to economic and social history and incorporate them into the wider picture advocated by the *annalistes*. The attention paid to economic history in the Cambridge history Tripos had opened my eyes to its value, and in any event anyone interested in seventeenth-century Spain could hardly ignore the problem of the country's 'decline', on which economic historians had produced important work.

I did not, however, see myself grappling with price and wage statistics, and found myself casting around for a rather less austere – and no doubt less rigorous – approach to the Spain of Philip IV. One of the few general books on the period was by an amateur British historian, Martin Hume, whose *The Court of Philip IV: Spain in Decadence* was first published in 1907 and reprinted twenty years later. Hume (1843–1910) was descended on his mother's side from Andrew Hume, an entrepreneur who had been recruited to promote manufacturing in the Spain of Carlos III, where he took up permanent residence. The young Martin Sharp, as he then was, first visited his Spanish relatives in 1860, and became an immediate and life-long Hispanophile. When the last of his Spanish relations died in 1876, he inherited their family property, which made him a man of independent means, and he assumed the name of Hume. After dabbling in business, politics and journalism, he drifted into writing about Spain and Anglo-Spanish relations. His publications earned him a growing reputation, but not, to his disappointment, a university chair. He was, and remained, an amateur, whose books, while drawing on his own archival researches and his first-hand knowledge of Spain, were written with the general public very much in mind.[3]

Hume's *The Court of Philip IV*, although in many ways an exasperating book, proved a useful introduction to the period. While Hume had a penchant for the melodramatic and the picturesque, he had explored the archives to good effect, and his book provided me with some useful leads. When looking up his publications I came across an article he had written for a Spanish periodical in 1907 on 'the centralizing policies of the Conde-Duque'.[4] In this article he depicts the Count of Olivares as a man determined to save an exhausted Spain from disaster. In the early years of the new reign he produced for the young king a lengthy memorandum outlining what, in his view, should be his governing principles.[5] The dominant theme of this document, according to Hume, was 'centralization'. For Olivares, a Spain divided into different kingdoms and territories was no match for a united France. His plans for reform included a proposal for unifying the country under royal control. This proposal, too hastily imposed and implemented, would set him on a collision course with the various kingdoms and provinces that made up the Iberian peninsula: the Basque provinces, Portugal, and the territories of the Crown of Aragon – the kingdoms of Aragon and Valencia, and the principality of Catalonia – all of them anxious to preserve themselves from domination by the Iberian heartland of Castile.

Reading this article made me realize that I had found the subject for which I was looking. I would study the Count-Duke of Olivares and his programme for reform. It is hard to know exactly what attracted me to the subject, but I suspect that, at some level, I was influenced by what was happening in my native land. Britain had emerged from the Second World War victorious but at the same time drastically weakened by the costs of the conflict, and I came to maturity at a time when the Attlee government was using the power of the state to push through an ambitious programme for recovery and reform. Like many others of my generation I was excited by the achievements of the immediate post-war years, but by the time I was embarking on my research in 1952–3 some of the weaknesses of the post-war settlement were already becoming apparent, and Attlee had fallen from power in 1951. Admiration for reform was coupled in my mind with an awareness of the loss of empire and intimations of national decline. It was difficult not to see similarities between the situation of Spain in the 1620s and that of Britain in the 1950s: an exhausted imperial power and a reforming government, followed by disappointed expectations and at least the partial failure of reform. Was my own country going the way of Spain?

The prospect of archival research on such a potentially promising subject was exciting, although I was momentarily shaken by a letter from Fernand Braudel. I had taken the precaution of writing to ask him what he felt about the subject I had chosen, and his reply was discouraging. He thought that, in the present state of historical research, it was 'not entirely reasonable' for me to dedicate my efforts to the 'ideological and practical origins of the Count-Duke's policy of administrative consolidation. It is a very difficult subject to delimit and grasp, and one whose general conclusions can be guessed in advance.' He explained that he had hesitated to give me such 'categorical advice', and trusted that I would have 'the wisdom, after reflection', to follow or not to follow it.[6] This response, from a historian whose work I enormously admired, came as something of a shock.

I consulted Herbert Butterfield, who displayed, both then and later, gifts of intuition which made him, as far as I was concerned, an ideal research supervisor, although he claimed no expertise in Spanish history. Somehow he seemed to have an instinctive feel for the kind of problems that were likely to arise, and he wrote admirable letters of encouragement and advice when the going seemed particularly hard. As a historian who himself was a pioneer in the development of new fields like the history of historiography and the history of science, he was always insistent on the need for flexibility, and on the impossibility of producing a 'definitive' work. 'All histories', he wrote to me on one occasion at an early stage in my research, 'are interim reports – and the question would be: can you get us a step forward?' On this occasion, he argued against Braudel that it did not really matter if general conclusions could be guessed in advance. It was much more important to explore a subject in depth and reconstruct how and why events developed as they did. It was for me to follow my own 'hunch' – a word he often used.[7]

Butterfield's advice served as an early lesson, and one that I would take to heart. He taught me, too, to appreciate the role of personality and contingency in shaping the past. In spite of Braudel's admonition, my instinct told me to persevere. Still in England, I spent my first year of research improving my Spanish, reading as many secondary and primary sources as I could find, and engaging in my first encounters with seventeenth-century Spanish handwriting in the extensive collection of Spanish documents held in the British Museum, from where, many years later, they would be transferred to the new British Library. Among the documents I consulted was the copy of Olivares's memorandum of instruction for the young King Philip IV that had inspired Martin Hume to write his article. As I handled the document, I felt myself for the first time in real touch with the past. I was ready and eager to set off for Spain and embark on serious research.

I left for the continent in the late summer of 1953, travelling across France by train to Barcelona, and carrying with me letters of introduction to one or two Catalan historians written for me by a well-known Catalan exile living in Cambridge, Dr Josep M. Batista i Roca (1895–1978), with whom I had discussed my research project on a number of occasions. From Barcelona I went to Madrid, on my way to the great castle-archive of Simancas, a short bus journey away from the city of Valladolid, where I settled into an inexpensive *pensión*. In those days there were very few researchers in the archives, and the director and the archive staff made every effort to be helpful to a young foreigner with still very inadequate Spanish. The castle of Simancas itself, dominating the small village of that name on the high Castilian plateau, made, and still makes, a deep impression, in spite of some unfortunate building works in recent years (Plate 2). We researchers would cross the bridge over the deep but dry moat and announce our presence by banging on the castle gate with its heavy iron knocker, scorching to the touch in the heat of the afternoon sun by the time we arrived for the evening session. The gate would be opened, and the *investigadores* would troop upstairs and take their places at the small tables in the *sala de investigadores*. Here the porters would come and go, carrying and delivering, with varying degrees of surliness or goodwill, the bundles of docu-ments, tied up with red ribbons, that had been requested. The bundles themselves were still stored on the pinewood shelves installed when Philip II decreed that the castle should become the permanent repository of Spanish state papers.

History was all around me at Simancas, and nobody with any sense of the past could fail to imbibe its atmosphere. There is an excitement about opening a bundle of documents for the first time, not really knowing what to expect, especially in Simancas where such catalogues as then existed tended to be very summary. The coming of digitization has meant that many historians today never get to see or handle the documents they consult, and if this has brought a new accessibility to myriads of documents, it has also taken away a form of direct contact with the past that nothing can quite replace. The sight, the touch and even the smell of sixteenth- or seventeenth-century documents, the dried brown ink, the paper itself sometimes crumbling in one's hand – all these sensory qualities enhanced, at least in my own experience, that imaginative and intuitive sense which is so important for the historical reconstruction of past societies.

Yet if I felt excitement in those first weeks in Simancas, I also felt a sense of growing frustration. I called up bundle after bundle of state papers for the 1620s, but none of them contained the kind of material that I had confidently expected to find. Foreign policy during the early years of the reign of Philip IV was well represented, but of the papers I was looking for, on domestic reform and 'centralization', I could find no trace. I knew from reading Marañón that the king gave Olivares permission to keep any state papers of interest to him that related to his time in office, but Marañón had nothing to say about the eventual fate of these documents. Although the Count-Duke made elaborate provisions for the permanent preservation of the great library that he assembled during his years in power, it was broken up very soon after his death in 1645. Many of his books were sold, some of them by his widow to pay for masses for his soul, while part at least of his archive eventually passed by descent to the Dukes of Alba. After two or three weeks of growing despair, I chanced on a guide to the family archive which the current Duke of Alba had recently published, and read there, to my horror, that the entire collection, with the exception of a single volume, was destroyed in two fires in the ducal palace of Buenavista in Madrid in 1794 and 1795. The bottom had fallen out of my subject even before I had begun.

This is the kind of problem, even if it does not always assume quite such a dramatic form, that is all too liable to confront even the best prepared of researchers. After an apparently ideal subject has finally been identified, it subsequently turns out, for one reason or another, to be simply not feasible. Such a situation calls for mental flexibility, and this is not easy to achieve when one has set one's heart on a subject. I was naturally devastated by my discovery, coming as it did at the beginning of what I had taken for granted would be a year of fruitful research in Spanish archives, replete with exciting discoveries. I could hardly return home empty-handed after less than three months in Spain, and was forced to think hard about possible ways of limiting my losses. As I did so, I reflected that in 1640 the Count-Duke's supposed 'centralizing' policies eventually led to rebellion in two of Philip IV's dominions, Catalonia and Portugal. Might it be possible to start at the other end, not with the central government in Madrid but with the rebellious territories themselves, and from there work back to discover what it was that led them to revolt?

I was faced with a choice, between Catalonia and Portugal, or, more prosaically, between the archives of Barcelona and

Lisbon. I chose Barcelona, in part because of my conversations with Batista i Roca, but largely because my immediate interest was in Spanish rather than Portuguese history. Portugal had been one of the dominions of the King of Spain since 1580, but the Portuguese succeeded in retaining the independence they won back in 1640, whereas the Catalans did not. The history of Catalonia, therefore, unlike that of Portugal, was, and continued to be, part of 'Spanish' history, and I was anxious not to be diverted from my country of choice. In the event, my decision to opt for Barcelona rather than Lisbon turned out to be fortunate. Although seventeenth-century Portugal offers many opportunities for study, little documentation has been found that would make it possible to unravel the many mysteries that still surround its rebellion.

In October 1953, therefore, I moved to Barcelona, where I was faced with a new challenge, this time linguistic. My Castilian was still not strong, but it soon became apparent that I would need to learn Catalan. Although the Franco regime was deeply hostile to the language, prohibiting its use for official business, banning it on the airwaves and in most publications, and forbidding its teaching in schools, it was everywhere spoken in Barcelona, where Catalan street names were changed into Castilian, or in some instances rigorously expunged. I clearly needed to learn the language if I wished to become acquainted with contemporary Catalonia, let alone understand the Catalonia of the seventeenth century. I decided that the best solution was to place a newspaper advertisement in *La Vanguardia*, to the effect that a young Englishman

wanted to live with a Barcelona family in order to learn
Catalan. I was deluged with replies, and finally identified a
sympathetic household (Plate 3). By insisting that the family
should only talk to me in Catalan I gradually acquired a
working knowledge of the language, and before my stay was
over I was even dreaming in Catalan.

Like Simancas, the Archive of the Crown of Aragon, at that
time located in the old viceregal palace in the Gothic Quarter
of Barcelona, exuded atmosphere, and this time I found documentation in abundance. The consultative body in Madrid
with overall responsibility for the government of the Principality
of Catalonia was the Council of Aragon, and from around
1600, in addition to extensive correspondence, there was a rich
series of documents, known as *consultas*, in which the members
of the Council discussed the issues of the day and laid out their
recommendations for the monarch. This made it possible to
reconstruct the decision-making process in Madrid from the
early seventeenth century onwards, and it became clear to me
that, in order to get a full understanding of the origins of the
1640 revolt, I would need to take the story back into the years
before the advent of Olivares to power in 1621.

I was soon deeply immersed in my subject, and with such an
abundance of documentation that by the end of the year I was
beginning to wonder whether I was not being too ambitious
and taking on more than I could handle, especially with only
another five or six months to go before returning home and
embarking on the writing of my dissertation. There is always a
danger that the chase for documents becomes an end in itself,

and Herbert Butterfield was insistent on the importance of getting down to writing instead of succumbing to the temptation of continuously collecting. As I explored the libraries and archives of Barcelona, I had begun to realize that, in the 1640 Catalan rebellion, I had stumbled on a highly promising topic, which would demand far more than six to nine months of research if its possibilities were to be exploited to the full.

The topic in itself was hardly new. The 1640 revolt, traditionally known as the *Guerra dels Segadors* after the peasants, or reapers, who came to Barcelona every summer to hire themselves out for the harvest season and who on this occasion brought rebellion with them, had long been identified as a decisive event in Catalonia's chequered history. It was central to the grand narrative elaborated by Catalan historians of the nineteenth and early twentieth centuries, a narrative in which Catalonia was depicted as the victim of continuous oppression by Castile.[8] As soon as I immersed myself in the papers of the Council of Aragon I began to feel doubts about this interpretation of events. Was Olivares really determined to destroy the traditional laws and liberties of the Principality at a critical moment in Spain's war with France, and did he deliberately provoke rebellion in Catalonia in the spring and summer of 1640, as nationalist historians argued, in order to have a pretext for reducing the Principality to subjection? There were some arguments in favour of this interpretation, but I felt that the whole question cried out for reappraisal, and it seemed to me that, as a historian who was neither Catalan nor Castilian but a genuine outsider, I might be in a position to make a contribution that would be both useful and impartial.

I was encouraged in this belief by Professor Jaume Vicens Vives (1910–60), the charismatic Professor of Modern History at Barcelona University, who invited me to come and talk to him when he found out what I was doing. Vicens, who had gathered around him a small group of pupils, some of whom I was getting to know during my sessions in the archive, had long been engaged in his own reappraisal of the history of late medieval Catalonia, and was also now deeply involved in studying the more recent Catalan past. I was welcomed into his group, which would meet every week, primarily to discuss the entries for the next issue of a journal he had launched, the *Índice Histórico Español*, a bibliographical record of new publications across the whole field of Spanish history. But these discussions ranged widely, across history, art and politics, and were, for me, an education in themselves.

I had become aware, however, that I had entered very sensitive territory. History and politics were not easily divorced, and nationalism, although pushed underground by the oppressive policies of the Franco regime, was a powerful emotion in the Catalonia of the 1950s, as it is today. As a historian, it was important for me to preserve my intellectual independence, and avoid being seduced, on the one hand, by the revisionist aspirations of Vicens and his followers, and, on the other, by my natural sympathy for an oppressed people. It was a tricky balancing act, and I cannot claim to have been consistently successful in preserving my stance.

At that moment I was more concerned to accumulate sufficient material for the writing of a thesis than with the interpretation I would eventually adopt when the time came to read through and organize my notes. After a brief return trip to Simancas in a search for material that I might previously have overlooked, I went back to England in the late spring of 1954 and settled down to write a dissertation. This was, in the first instance, to be a dissertation for a prize fellowship at Trinity College, and for six weeks I battered out on my typewriter nearly a thousand pages on 'Castile and Catalonia, 1621–40'. I had accumulated far more material than I had ever realized. The dissertation, although far too long, won me a prize fellowship, and with it the opportunity, if I so wished, for four years of uninterrupted research. In the event, these amounted to no more than two, since I was appointed a teaching fellow of my college in 1956, and a university assistant lecturer in the following year. But the fellowship enabled me to return to Spain for the best part of a year in 1955–6 in order to extend and deepen my research, before writing up my findings for a doctoral thesis – at that time limited to a mere 60,000 words – and then, in due course, preparing them for publication as a book.

That additional year proved to be of immense importance for my continuing personal discovery of Spain. I returned to the archive of Simancas for the hot summer months of 1955, taking off at weekends to visit cities and towns of the Castilian interior. On arriving in Simancas I found that a modest residence for the use of *investigadores* had just been opened, almost opposite the castle, and I may well have been its first occupant. In due course I was joined there by one or two others, and in particular by a tall, sallow-faced historian from Granada, Antonio Domínguez Ortiz (1909–2003), at that time still relatively unknown and little appreciated outside a small circle of specialists, but who was to become the most eminent Spanish historian of Habsburg Spain in the last decades of the twentieth century. His knowledge of the social and political history of the period was already vast, and at that time he was embarking on a study of the finances of the Spanish crown during the reign of Philip IV. Ironically, this was the subject that Fernand Braudel urged me to make the principal topic of my research, first in our exchange of letters and subsequently when I called on him in Paris while on my way to Spain.

I enjoyed many long conversations with Domínguez Ortiz over our unappetizing lunches and dinners in the *residencia*, and he was generous in placing at my disposal the information he had amassed during many years of research in Spain's archives. From him I learned much, not only about the history of his country, but also about its current problems, and the difficulties that faced Spanish scholars, most of whom had neither the resources nor the opportunities for serious research, and were too busy trying to earn a living by teaching and writing to find time to settle down to work in the archives. His own life exemplified many of these difficulties, if anything in an extreme form, although, by sheer force of determination, he succeeded in transcending them. Neither then nor later did he secure a university appointment, and his professional career was confined to institutes of higher education. Recognition, when it came, came first from abroad, and only in his later years did his own country belatedly follow suit.[9]

As a foreigner during these grim Franco years I was in a privileged position, as I increasingly came to appreciate, enjoying the luxury of time and financial resources of which young Spanish scholars of my generation, and even their elders, could only dream. Few of them had the opportunity for foreign travel and for learning foreign languages beyond the borders of their own country; and their access to foreign works of history was limited both by censorship and by price. Marxist publications were banned, as were any books on contemporary Spain that were judged to be unfavourable to the regime. Foreign scholars like myself, free to come and go as they wished, and with open access to the latest international scholarship, were therefore presented with an almost open field for research. I, for one, was determined to make the most of the opportunities that came my way, while at the same time hoping that one day I would be in a position to repay the country that had received me with such generosity by adding my own personal contribution to the understanding and interpretation of its history, for both a Spanish and a foreign public.

Having spent so much time reading the official documents generated by the ministers and agents of the Olivares regime, I was becoming uneasily aware that I might have been getting only one side of the story of the origins of the revolt of the Catalans. It was essential for me to return to Catalonia, and try to immerse myself more deeply in municipal and ecclesiastical records which might help to give me a clearer idea of how seventeenth-century Catalans viewed their own situation. I therefore returned to Barcelona in the autumn of 1955. This time I took up residence with a different family. The son of the house, a young doctor, had a wide circle of contacts among Barcelona's professional and cultural elite, and in his company I acquired a feel for twentieth-century Catalonia and its problems while deepening my knowledge of its seventeenth-century past.

Working in the various archives and libraries of Barcelona, and making periodic excursions to towns whose archives, as far as I could discover in advance, had survived the disruptions and destruction caused by the Civil War, I was gradually able, as I had hoped, to piece together the complex picture of a seventeenth-century society divided within itself, and reacting in anger and bewilderment to the pressures emanating from a royal government that was determined to mobilize its resources for war. Fascinating letters and papers came to light, including the diary of a Barcelona lawyer and chronicler, which would give me some striking insights into the mentality of a member of the professional classes and into his attitudes towards Castilians and his fellow Catalans.[10] Archival research inevitably involves much tedium as document after document yields nothing of special interest, but this kind of discovery, suddenly opening as it does new windows onto the past, more than compensates for those long hours spent trawling to little or no effect through bundles of dusty or crumbling papers, many of them written in crabbed or indecipherable hands.

My wanderings round Catalonia and my encounters with local archivists and historians were enjoyable in themselves, and sometimes led me into curious situations, as when a canon of the cathedral chapter of the Seu d'Urgell, in the foothills of the Catalan Pyrenees, agreed to let me work in the cathedral archive as long as his fellow canons, with whom his relations were obviously not of the best, remained unaware of my presence. He would lock me into the archive for the morning and I had the run of it to myself – on one occasion for rather too long, since he forgot to let me out at lunchtime. Historians should be as much concerned with the present as with the past, and such encounters and incidents gave me sudden and unexpected glimpses into aspects of Catalan life in the middle decades of the twentieth century. They also enhanced my understanding of Catalan society in an earlier age. The canons of seventeenth-century Urgell, as I came to appreciate when I worked on the papers in their archive, had a factious history.

At times, indeed, it seemed to me as if past and present were inextricably entangled. One day I made the mistake of asking a Barcelona traffic policeman for directions in Catalan instead of Castilian. His response was, 'Speak the language of the empire [Hable la lengua del imperio]'. It was the very phrase I had read a few weeks earlier in a pamphlet of the 1630s on the language to be employed in sermons, in which the author attacked the Catalans for not speaking the 'language of the empire'. It seemed as though, in spite of the passage of three centuries, time had stood still.

It became clear to me in the course of my researches that the complex nature of the relationship between Castile and Catalonia since the union of the crowns of Castile and Aragon in the late fifteenth century offered a vital clue to the understanding not merely of Catalan history, but of that of Spain as a whole. Castile, as the heartland of the Iberian peninsula, became its dominant region in the sixteenth century, and when Philip II chose Madrid as the permanent seat of his court in 1561, his choice of capital reinforced Castilian predominance and gave the apparatus of state power a distinctively Castilian cast. But Castile was not Spain, although at times the attitudes of members of the Castilian governing class gave the impression, particularly to non-Castilians, that they regarded Spain and Castile as interchangeable political entities. The arrogance of a people who had come to regard themselves as predestined to rule an empire aroused intense resentment in other parts of the peninsula. A sixteenth-century Catalan alleged that the Castilians 'want to be so absolute, and put so high a value on their own achievements and so low a value on everyone else's, that they give the impression that they alone are descended from heaven, and the rest of mankind are mud'.[11] The impression would not be erased.

My seventeenth-century researches and mid-twentieth-century travels brought home to me the enduring diversity of a Spain on which the regime of General Franco was doing its best to impose a centralizing uniformity. I saw here some striking parallels with the policies of the Olivares regime three centuries earlier. The history of Spain appeared to consist of a never-ending conflict between the country's inherent diversity and an insistent pressure from the centre for unity. On the one hand there were the different kingdoms and provinces of the peninsula – the territories of the Crown of Aragon, the Basque provinces, Navarre, and, between 1580 and 1640, Portugal – and on the other a central administration which, over many centuries, was committed to the upholding of dynastic or state interests and of a set of transcendental values which it saw itself as divinely appointed to defend.

The seventeenth-century confrontation between the Principality of Catalonia and the government of Philip IV in Madrid seemed to me at once to highlight and epitomize this continuing and unresolved tension between unity and diversity. Perhaps influenced by the sociological models of the day, I cast my story in terms of the struggle between centre and periphery, which in retrospect can be seen as a rather crude formulation of an always complex process of negotiation and conflict in which the dividing lines were rarely clear-cut. This theme of centre and periphery ran not only through my dissertation, which was eventually published in 1963 under the title *The Revolt of the Catalans*, but also through *Imperial Spain, 1469–1716*, a book which I published in the same year.[12] This arose out of the first set of lectures I delivered as a young assistant lecturer in the Cambridge History Faculty, and was commissioned by the publishers to fill a gap in the textbook market. The choice of dates was itself emblematic: 1469, the year of the marriage of Ferdinand and Isabella that would lead to the union of the Crowns of Castile and Aragon, and 1716, when the new Bourbon dynasty that came to the throne in

1700 decreed the so-called '*Nueva Planta*', which abolished the traditional laws and liberties of the territories of the Crown of Aragon. Emblematic also was the quotation from the Spanish philosopher Ortega y Gasset with which the book ended: 'Castile has made Spain, and Castile has destroyed it.' My *Imperial Spain* was, at least in part, the story of the defeat of the periphery by the centre, of the Crown of Aragon by Castile.

I was not to know when I published the book that fifteen years later, following the death of Franco in 1975 and Spain's transition to democracy, its new constitution would officially recognize the country's diversity and transfer many of the competencies of the central government to the various regions and provinces, which were now styled 'autonomous communities'. *Imperial Spain* was published at a time when the country was still tightly held in the grip of an authoritarian regime which endlessly repeated its message of unity, order and a continuing fidelity to spiritual values on which it alleged that the rest of the world had turned its back. When the book was originally published, it was with a purely Anglo-American readership in mind, and, without giving it much thought, I added the euphonious word 'Imperial' to the title after the publishers had asked for something more distinctive than simply 'Spain' with a couple of dates. For some reason it never crossed my mind that I had chosen for the book a title that conformed perfectly to the ideology of the Franco regime. When it was published in Spanish two years later as *La España imperial*, readers in Spain would naturally have expected a historical textbook that ran along conventional lines. Once they began to read, they found themselves faced with something rather different.

Inevitably I wrote the book as an outsider, not as an insider. I brought to it not only the findings of my own specialist researches into the relationship between seventeenth-century Catalonia and Madrid, but also the results of my immersion in modern British and European historiography during the preceding ten to fifteen years. Unconstrained by the traditions of Spanish historical writing, and benefiting from the wide range of literature freely accessible to me, I approached my assignment from the standpoint of a historian of the new, post-Second World War generation, very much alive to the historiographical and other preoccupations of his own times. This meant that I addressed my central theme of the rise and fall of Spain as the dominant European power with the conviction that it could not be properly treated purely in terms of political, diplomatic and military history, but that it also demanded due consideration of the nature of Spanish society and of the economic and financial imperatives that helped to determine Spain's imperial trajectory.

Such an approach would hardly have come as a novelty to British or American readers, but it struck Spaniards, cocooned in their suffocating authoritarian straitjacket, in a very different light. Although this was not my intention, the ideologically correct title turned out to be no more than a cover for a number of subversive messages. Of these, the theme of unity and diversity was no doubt the most disturbing in official eyes. But the emphasis on social and economic history, although far from Marxist in character, seems also to have come as something of a revelation, even though major Spanish historians of the period, like Ramón Carande (1887–1986), working in Seville on the finances of Charles V, were making important contributions in just those fields. They did not, however, figure prominently in the standard textbooks used in Spanish universities at the time, which remained resolutely positivist in their tone, and heavily weighted towards political, military and diplomatic history. Although *Imperial Spain* was in many respects a brash and premature attempt to provide a synthesis, it had the merit of looking at the period with fresh eyes, and suggested a history still open to consideration, rather than one closed off and embalmed. Not surprisingly, it enjoyed a great success in Spain and was read by generation after generation of university students.

As I came to appreciate when writing *The Revolt of the Catalans* and *Imperial Spain*, a historian has advantages as well as disadvantages in studying the history of a society that is not his or her own. The disadvantages are obvious enough. There are some features of a foreign society that it is always difficult or even impossible for an outsider to comprehend fully. For a northern Protestant like myself, Mediterranean Catholicism, with its strong devotion to images, is bound to seem alien and inaccessible. It is difficult, too, for those brought up in the nuclear families of the north to appreciate the importance of the extended family in Spanish society and the intensity of Spanish family life, at least as it was lived up to and including the middle years of the twentieth century. On the other hand, looking in with fresh eyes from the outside, the foreigner is well placed to notice features so familiar to natives that they pay them no attention. In working on Catalonia, for instance, I was struck by the layout of the *masia*, the form of traditional farmstead that still dots the countryside, and by the way in which the *masia* shaped the sense of family and inheritance in Catalan rural society.[13] The topic was so familiar to Catalans that it still lacked adequate study at the time when I was undertaking my research, although Vicens Vives, in the lectures I attended at Barcelona University, made a point of emphasizing its critical importance for understanding the special combination of rural stability and economic dynamism that would do so much to shape Catalan society.

Historians of a society other than their own confront the problem that famously faces anthropologists also – how to understand and interpret that society while being in it but not of it. In some respects, indeed, the dilemma for historians is double, since they are dealing with societies distant from themselves not only in space but also in time. This affects even historians studying the history of their own country, since, in L. P. Hartley's famous words, 'the past is a foreign country', and apparent similarities between past and present can be a deadly snare. The question is one that has exercised the minds of many anthropologists, not least that of Clifford Geertz, who was to be my colleague and friend in the years I would spend as a member of the Faculty at the Institute for Advanced Study in Princeton between 1973 and 1990. In one of his characteristically coruscating essays Geertz, discussing the posthumously published *Diary* of Bronislaw Malinowski, remarked that its contents 'rendered established accounts of how anthropologists work fairly well implausible. The myth of the chameleon fieldworker, perfectly self-tuned to his exotic surroundings, a walking miracle of empathy, tact, patience, and cosmopolitanism, was demolished by the man who had perhaps done most to create it.'[14]

While insisting on the continuing importance of the anthropologist's clinging to the injunction 'to see things from the native's point of view', Geertz sought to resolve the dilemma in his own fieldwork by 'searching out and analysing the symbolic forms – words, images, institutions, behaviors – in terms of which . . . people actually represented themselves to themselves and to one another'.[15] The historians who have most successfully interpreted the history of foreign societies have always sought to do this, although Geertz's own example has enhanced the attention paid in recent historical writing to symbols and ceremonial actions. The only way to obtain at least some understanding of a society other than one's own is to develop antennae sufficiently sensitive to pick up even the most remote signals, however faint.

No doubt this demands a prior capacity to listen, and the study of foreign societies is not for the tone-deaf. But, at least to judge from my own experience, the capacity to listen can be enhanced by a willingness to blend into the background whenever possible, endeavouring to assimilate some of the modes of thought and behaviour of the surrounding society. This is not a question of seeking to abandon one's own identity so much as of acquiring an additional identity, almost like a second garment, and this is a process that works best when it is least self-conscious.

British historians over the past two centuries have perhaps done more than their fair share of studying the history of foreign countries, for reasons that have yet to be fully explained.[16] The possession of overseas empire, with the accompanying need to understand the mentality and customs of peoples who had become the subjects of the British crown, undoubtedly stimulated an interest in 'the Other', as well as creating a practical demand for men and women, whether government officials, anthropologists, or even historians, who could interpret and explain the behaviour of these peoples to their new imperial masters. If their interpretations were frequently condescending, they nevertheless sprang from deep knowledge and intensive study of the societies in which they had immersed and, sometimes, lost themselves. In addition to the demands of empire, many Britons between the mid-eighteenth and the mid-twentieth centuries were encouraged by curiosity, the love of adventure, and sometimes pure eccentricity to explore a world beyond their own. Whether more of them possessed these characteristics than their continental or North American contemporaries is far from clear, and their inner motivations are likely to remain a mystery. In some cases at least, engagement with 'the Other' may have served as the means to help them discover themselves.

Whether my own was one of these cases I am still, half a century later, unable to say, but I do know that the attempt to understand a society or societies remote in space and time was, and has continued to be, a source of intense personal enjoyment. There is always a sense of excitement about setting foot on unknown or uncharted territory and unlocking its secrets. That sense of excitement is likely to be familiar to any historian who solves a historical riddle or uncovers a previously unknown piece of evidence, but it may well be particularly powerful when it also involves the discovery of a foreign land. Here, the very fact of foreignness makes the code doubly indecipherable, and the satisfaction of breaking the cypher all the greater. But the test, as with all historical writing, is the plausibility of the result, and the way in which it is communicated to others.

Effective communication, both to Spaniards and to non-Spaniards, seemed to me all the more important where the history of Spain was concerned. In the earlier periods of its history, at the time when it still enjoyed the status of a great power, Spain was notoriously sensitive to alleged misrepresentations and to slights to its reputation by foreign writers. The Black Legend – the *leyenda negra* – of Spanish cruelty and fanaticism, constructed in the sixteenth century in response to the activities of the Inquisition and the perpetration of atrocities in Europe and America, drove the governments of Philip II and his successors onto the defensive. In the eighteenth century a royal decree banned the translation and circulation of William Robertson's *History of America*, after it had initially been welcomed in Spanish scholarly circles.[17]

The effect of the Black Legend, as constructed and diffused by foreign enemies, was not confined to official circles. By degrees it seared its way also into the national psyche.[18] Yet although the sensitivity to foreign criticism continued into the twentieth century, and was still very much alive in the age of Franco, there had developed alongside it a vein of self-criticism which itself can be traced back to the sixteenth century, when Bartolomé de las Casas and others denounced the cruelties perpetrated by their compatriots against the indigenous peoples of America. This self-criticism became increasingly vocal in the later eighteenth and nineteenth centuries as Spanish intellectuals contemplated their country's apparent inability to keep pace, whether culturally or politically, with the more 'advanced' European societies.[19]

Such self-criticism led some of them to appreciate the activities of foreign scholars who studied and illuminated aspects of Spanish history and civilization that Spaniards themselves had, for one reason or another, failed to address. Their characteristically generous response helped to create an image that seems to have no exact equivalent in other European countries. This is the image of the *hispanista* – the foreign scholar who devotes his or her life to understanding and interpreting Spain.[20]

As far as the study of history is concerned, the phenomenon of 'Hispanism' can be seen, at least in part, as the expression of a feeling that foreign scholars might be able to make up for some of the deficiencies of native scholarship. In practice, perceptions of the backwardness of Spanish scholarship did not necessarily accord with the reality. Twentieth-century Spain produced some highly distinguished historians, some of whom were reaching the height of their powers at the time when I was embarking on my researches. These included the economic historians Ramón Carande and Felipe Ruiz Martín (1915–2004), the intellectual and cultural historian José Antonio Maravall (1911–86), and the two historians who most influenced my own work, Vicens Vives and Domínguez Ortiz. But the difficulties affecting historical research in the period of international isolation following the Civil War tended to emphasize the deficiencies and weaknesses of Spanish historical writing, and made the contributions of the so-called 'Hispanists' all the more welcome.

Along with Raymond Carr and Hugh Thomas, both working on more modern periods, I was one of the beneficiaries of this willingness of Spanish scholars and the wider reading public to look at their national history through a foreign lens. It is to be hoped that this lens has not introduced too many new distortions of its own, but it did offer a national readership new perspectives on the country's past, not least by placing it in a wider European context at a time when the integration of Spain into the developing European community seemed to offer the best and, perhaps, the only hope for a better future.

My own efforts, particularly in *Imperial Spain*, were especially directed to contesting the essentialism to be found in so many discussions of Spain's past – the notion that the key to understanding the country's fortunes and misfortunes somehow lay hidden in the recesses of a Spanish collective psyche. For example, was the 'idleness' of seventeenth-century Spaniards, which drew so much criticism from contemporary Spaniards and foreign visitors alike, inherent in the Spanish character, or was it the outcome of the lack of opportunities for regular employment? Similar criticisms were in fact levelled at the population of sixteenth- and early seventeenth-century England. If the tendency to idleness was to be ascribed not to national characteristics but to those of pre-modern agrarian economies in general, then perhaps Spain was not as different as the conventional interpretation would have us believe.

Attempts to challenge the notion of a Spain that was somehow 'different' have helped Spaniards themselves to view their past in a fresh light. But in my own career I have been at least as concerned to reach a non-Spanish as a Spanish readership, for reasons that are similarly related to the image of Spain. The Black Legend may have etched itself into the Spanish psyche, but it has also had a profound impact on foreign and especially Anglo-American attitudes to the country. In the eighteenth century the *Encyclopédie* notoriously asked what Spain had done for Europe 'in the last two centuries, in the last four, or ten'.[21] Nearly two centuries later Kenneth Clark, in the preface to his *Civilisation*, the book that arose out of his famous television series, could still write that 'if I had been talking about the history of art, it would not have been possible to leave out Spain; but when one asks what Spain has done to enlarge the human mind and pull mankind a few steps up the hill, the answer is less clear. *Don Quixote*, the Great Saints, the Jesuits in South America? Otherwise she has simply remained Spain.'[22] *Pace* Kenneth Clark, did the civilizing process really come to a halt at the Pyrenees?

The persistence of outmoded stereotypes of Spain, particularly in Britain and the United States, has resulted from the convergence of a number of elements. In part it is the consequence of religious and national antipathies that originated in the burning of the Protestant martyrs in the reign of Mary Tudor and the war between the Spain of Philip II and the England of Elizabeth I. Drawing on the literature generated by the Black Legend, and kept alive by national rivalries and fears of popish plots, the unfavourable perception of Spain was also a response to widespread European apprehensions that Habsburg Spain, as the dominant power in Europe, was aspiring to 'universal monarchy'. As Spain lost its international dominance these apprehensions disappeared, only to be replaced by a new set of images, as it became typecast as a backward, superstitious and fanatical country weighed down by centuries of misgovernment. In the nineteenth century, in Britain and the United States alike, racialist theories of Anglo-Saxon supremacy combined with traditional anti-Catholic attitudes to reinforce such images, while the political instability of Spain itself and of the Latin American nations recently emancipated from the long centuries of Spanish rule simply served to confirm what had always been believed about the dead hand of Spain's legacy.

The interpretation of Spain to a non-Spanish public therefore involves questioning and confronting a set of deeply entrenched stereotypes. The persistent challenge is to make Spain comprehensible to an international readership whose knowledge of the country may be limited to a few distorted images, or, alternatively, who may wonder why there is any need to bother with Spain at all. 'Why Spain?' was a question that I had to answer for myself even as I attempted to answer it for others. My own answer, as it has evolved over the years, is that this is an endlessly fascinating country whose history, made up of striking successes and equally striking failures, embraces topics of universal import. Here is a country and a people whose past saw the construction and subsequent deconstruction of complex religious and ethnic relationships as it stood poised between the worlds of Christianity, Judaism and Islam; a country that took the lead among European powers in conquering and governing a vast overseas empire, and that has persistently sought, and never quite succeeded, in reconciling the conflicting demands of unity and diversity on its own territory; and a country whose religious, cultural and artistic achievements over the course of the centuries have made an enormously rich if often controversial contribution to human civilization. Hispanism by itself is not enough. The figure of the 'Hispanist' should always take second place to that of the historian. But fortunate the historian whose chosen country has so much to offer!

CHAPTER TWO

National and transnational history

M Y immersion in Catalan history and Catalan society in the 1950s proved to be a rude awakening. Nothing in the first twenty years of my life as a middle-class mid-twentieth-century Englishman had even remotely prepared me for existence in a country without liberty, ruled by a dictatorial regime which even refused the right of many of its citizens to express themselves freely in their own language. Although Catalan was not entirely prohibited, its use was officially discouraged, as I found in my encounter with the Barcelona traffic policeman,[1] and a generation of children never learnt in school how to write the language that it spoke as a matter of course at home.

As a foreigner, it was the combination of censorship and prohibitions on the use of Catalan that most made me aware, on a daily basis, of the absence of freedom that was a fact of life for the Catalan population as a whole. Normal symbols of collective identity like the flag were outlawed, and repressed national sentiment had few outlets for expression other than the solemn traditional dance of the *sardana* (which required far too much mathematical calculation for my unmathematical mind), and the rowdy football matches that pitted Barcelona against Madrid. What perhaps brought home to me the intensity of national feeling was something that occurred during a walk in the countryside with the historian Ferran Soldevila (1894–1971) shortly after the beginning of my first period of residence in Catalonia. We were discussing seventeenth-century Catalan history, and I asked him to sing for me the song of the *segadors*, the harvesters whose arrival in Barcelona in June 1640 helped to transform the uprising in the countryside into a generalized revolt. This song, revised and reworked during the Catalan cultural revival – the *renaixença* – of the nineteenth century and strictly prohibited by the regime, had become Catalonia's national hymn, and as Soldevila sang one verse after another, the tears ran down his cheeks. As I listened to him while we walked, I realized, I think for the first time, what it really meant not to be free.

Soldevila had more reason than many to feel the sense of loss that came with the victory of Franco over the forces of the Republic. Exiled at the end of the Civil War he returned to Spain in 1943, but had to wait until his sixtieth year, in 1954, a few months after we took our country walk, to be allowed to return to the official corps of archivists. A historian of great learning, he had been a preeminent representative of

Catalan nationalist historiography in the years before the outbreak of the Civil War, and had published an impressive three-volume history of Catalonia in 1934–5.[2] In 1935 he was appointed director of the historical institute at the Autonomous University of Barcelona. The war destroyed both his career and his country, and, not surprisingly, he gave the impression of being a defeated man.

The contrast with Jaume Vicens Vives, with whom I was soon to establish close relations, could not have been sharper (Plate 4). Vicens exuded optimism, whereas Soldevila had about him an aura of ineffable sadness. The relations between the two men can best be described as respectful but cool. While still writing his doctoral thesis on the reign of Ferdinand II of Aragon, Vicens, sixteen years younger than Soldevila, was publishing work which openly challenged the approach of traditional Catalan historical writing that had arisen out of the Romantic movement and the nationalist revival of the nineteenth and early twentieth centuries. In 1935 Vicens was attacked in the press by a well-known historian, Antoni Rovira i Virgili, for his lack of Catalan 'sensibility', and a fierce public debate ensued in which Vicens countered by accusing historians attached to the traditionalist Institut d'Estudis Catalans, to which Soldevila belonged, of approaching the history of Catalonia with preconceived ideological views. In the same year he published a review of Soldevila's *Història de Catalunya* which criticized it for its neglect of economic and social history and represented it as the culmination of sixty years of historical writing dominated by a Romantic and nationalist approach.

Vicens therefore set out on his career as a revisionist historian, representing a new generation more in tune than its predecessor with the modern world, although, ironically, Soldevila before him had seen himself as breaking with the Romantic tradition of nineteenth-century writing and setting Catalan history on a more modern footing.[3] Like Soldevila, Vicens spent some difficult years in the immediate post-Civil War period, although, unlike him, he turned back before reaching the frontier in 1939 and decided to stay in his own country rather than go into exile. His decision inevitably involved compromises with the regime, which eventually rehabilitated him in 1947 and allowed him to return to university teaching.[4] As Professor of Modern History at Barcelona University he soon established himself as a dominant if controversial figure in Catalan cultural and political life, making it his mission to demythologize Catalan history and equip a new generation to rebuild the country and prepare it for the post-Franco era.

Since my own researches on the revolt of 1640 were leading me to question the interpretations of the nationalist school, I naturally found myself intellectually at home in the circle of Vicens and his pupils. Like them I became something of an iconoclast, anxious to dispel the myths. Inevitably there was an element of tension as I sought to reconcile my natural sympathy for an oppressed people with what I saw as my duty as a historian to reveal some of the less attractive facts I had uncovered about a traditionally glorious moment in the history of their country. Understandable fears for the survival of the *patria* went hand in hand with self-interest, and, not surprisingly, some of the leaders of the rebellion, who were firmly enshrined in the pantheon of nationalist historiography, turned out to have feet of clay. My findings came as a source of disappointment to Soldevila and his friends in the semi-clandestine Institut d'Estudis Catalans. They had naturally hoped that a presumably impartial foreign historian would vindicate their interpretation. Now it looked as though he might have sold out to the other side.

Such reactions made it impossible to ignore the fact that I had chosen to study, in a tense political environment, a highly sensitive subject – the perennial problem of the relationship between Madrid and the Catalans. It is indicative of the atmosphere in the Spain of the early 1950s that when Vicens Vives asked me to publish an advance of my findings in his newly founded historical journal, he eventually decided, after commissioning a Spanish translation, that my article should be left in the decent obscurity of the English language, although it remains unclear whether he was more concerned about government censorship or about the reactions my piece might provoke inside Catalonia itself.[5]

Any personal dilemmas of my own, however, although at times painful, were of little importance compared with the wider issues at stake. As I became increasingly aware, the disagreements between Soldevila and Vicens Vives were not peculiar to Catalonia, but were expressive of the tensions that are inherent in the writing of all national history, since every nation views its past through the prism of the present, and its present through the prism of the past. Because of this constant interaction between past and present, national historians consciously or unconsciously shape the image that nations have of themselves, and, by shaping it, become the largely hidden players in the unending drama of the politics of national identity.

A nation has famously been defined by Benedict Anderson as 'an imagined political community' – '*imagined* because the members of even the smallest nation will never know most of their fellow-members, meet them, or even hear of them, yet in the mind of each lives the image of their communion'.[6] That image creates, as it did in Catalonia, a sense of mutual solidarity in the face of neighbours and more distant peoples who, whether hostile or not, are perceived as being different. This in turn generates a sense of exceptionalism of the kind that is inherent in the self-perception of every national community.

As I became aware when writing *Imperial Spain*, the sense of exceptionalism is capable of creating a collective state of mind that might be described as the 'chosen nation syndrome'. Nations that succumb to this syndrome regard themselves as being entrusted by God with a providential mission which only they can discharge.[7] In seeing itself as being divinely appointed to defend, uphold and extend the cause of the Roman Church, sixteenth-century Spain provides a striking example of a nation in the grip of this syndrome, but it is far from being unique. Nineteenth-century Britain had no doubt of its privileged position in the eyes of the Lord, while the United States has notoriously shaped its self-image as the exemplification of 'manifest destiny'.

Although the sense of being a chosen nation can be a source of aggressive self-confidence, as it was for sixteenth-century Castilians, the national mood can easily turn sour if things begin to go wrong, and the mission falters or is seen to be failing. This change of mood was a theme that would come to occupy my attention as I examined the career of the Count-Duke of Olivares and the perception of decline in seventeenth-century Spain.[8] A once confident national community turns in on itself in a bout of introspection, while also feeling that the whole world is against it.

In this soul-searching it takes upon itself something of the 'innocent victim' syndrome that is all too prone to afflict nations possessed of a strong sense of their own exceptional character, but unable, for one reason or another, to achieve the status and the opportunities to which they feel themselves entitled. National communities that succumb to this syndrome tend to see themselves as permanent victims of malign forces emanating from a more powerful neighbour or neighbours. The memory of defeat by the Turks at the battle of Kosovo in 1389 has shaped the collective consciousness of the Serbs from that day to this. In the same way, nineteenth- and twentieth-century Catalans were encouraged to see their past as the story of a pernicious attempt by their Castilian neighbours, from the early fifteenth century onwards, to undermine their institutions and way of life, and eventually destroy their distinctive identity as a people.

Neither a chosen nation syndrome nor an innocent victim syndrome is conducive to the writing of good history. The first encourages an approach to the past conceived in essentialist terms, whereby national successes are seen as deriving from the special characteristics – spiritual, biological or racial – inherent in a people, and directed to the achievement of the goals they have defined for themselves within a framework of providential or messianic thinking. The effect of the second is to impute all the community's misfortunes to others and to ignore or disregard failings closer to home.

This was the state of mind that Vicens Vives set out to challenge in his attempt to reappraise and rewrite the history of Catalonia – an attempt that was partially frustrated by his premature death in 1960, although his message resonated with important sections of Catalan society, and had lasting consequences for the way in which Catalan history was written. Vicens saw the sense of victimhood as a corrosive element in Catalan society, and one that impeded its ability to address some of its most pressing problems. The study of the past demanded a clear-sighted approach, based on all the available evidence as impartially presented as humanly possible – an approach that would not shrink from pointing out, where necessary, the defects, the disagreements and the internal divisions that had sometimes made the Catalans their own worst enemies when faced with challenges.

Such a dispelling of national myths is integral to the historical enterprise, and it was natural for me to share Vicens's outlook and see myself as a companion in arms. *The Revolt of the Catalans* was strongly marked by a determination to free the history of seventeenth-century Catalonia from the grip of nationalist mythology. As an anonymous reviewer of the book in the *Times Literary Supplement* observed, 'there is little room here for romantic idealization of a nationalist movement. The motives of the rebels were at best confused, at worst merely self-interested, and only one of them – Pau Claris, who unhappily died in 1641 – appears to have been a leader of any stature.'[9]

I naturally like to think that I struck the right balance, and Charles Boxer, the distinguished historian of the Iberian and Dutch worlds who would later be a colleague at King's College, London, gratifyingly commented that I had been 'admirably fair to all parties in this tangled story'.[10] Reviews in Spain itself were favourable, with one Catalan reviewer asserting that 'in general' I 'embraced the Catalan cause',[11] but some of my findings were distinctly unpalatable in Catalonia. More recently, with the resurgence of more radical forms of Catalan nationalism, historians of a new generation have seen an anti-Catalan bias in the book and have criticized me for writing top-down history from the standpoint of the man on horseback, the Count-Duke in Madrid.[12] No doubt, if I had written the book half a century later, I would have written it rather differently, and would certainly have done more to dispel the erroneous impression that I saw Olivares as standing for the future and the Catalans for the past. On the other hand, I believe that the book sets the Catalan revolt and its early seventeenth-century background within a coherent narrative framework that still holds good, and its publication undoubtedly encouraged later generations of Catalan historians to follow up some of my leads and explore in greater depth the economic, social and personal tensions that I had detected in a divided Catalonia.

As an outsider to Catalonia I of course had less emotional involvement in the reassessment of the country's past than native historians like Vicens Vives and his pupils. The same may also hold true of the remarkable French Marxist historian Pierre Vilar (1906–2003), who during the period of my research was completing his great if only partially realized work on the origins of Catalonia as a modern industrial society, and was generous in lending me the sections dealing with seventeenth-century Catalonia in his as yet unpublished book.[13] Vilar, however, writing about a later period, had a more positive story to tell. In general, native historians are more likely than outsiders to be aware of the degree to which a revisionist approach to national history involves losses as well as gains. Imagined communities are shaped in large part by a shared recollection of the past, and societies deprived of cherished memories are threatened by a loosening of the ties that bind them together. To the extent that those memories are wrapped within myths and legends, there are understandable grounds for anxiety about what will happen to the solidarity of the national community when its past is stripped of legends.

This is a legitimate fear, but the consequences of clinging too tightly to an invented or distorted past can all too easily lead to disaster. In the hands of unscrupulous politicians, like those who led the Serbs to defeat in the closing years of the twentieth century, the manipulation of a national history built on myth becomes a device for mobilizing the population in defence of a misconceived cause. In this instance the sense of innocent victimhood, nurtured by the historical myths that had grown up around the battle of Kosovo, became a pretext for the committing of horrific atrocities against neighbours who were represented as determined to destroy everything the Serbs had achieved since the early nineteenth century when they first broke the bonds of Turkish domination.[14]

While the history of the Serbs, as of other Balkan nationalities, offers a stark reminder of the potentially disastrous consequences of national myth transmuted into national history, this may well seem an extreme case when set against the innumerable instances of apparently harmless contributions to the forging of a sense of national identity. The image of the Pilgrim Fathers and of a shining city on a hill has for generations been central to the self-image of the United States. What could provide a more benign rallying call to national action than this image, as deployed by President Reagan? Like all such images, however, that of the Pilgrim Fathers and the settlement of New England is necessarily selective. As I came to appreciate when I later turned my attention to the history of colonial North America for my book *Empires of the Atlantic World*, it steps lightly over the prior settlement of Jamestown and plays down the massive contribution of Virginia and the American South, with their own distinctive values, to the making of the society that was to emerge from the British colonization of North America. Similarly it leaves little or no space for the incorporation into the national narrative of Native Americans and imported Africans, without whom the evolution of the colonies into the United States as we know it today would have been profoundly different.[15]

Sooner or later the alternative narratives will force their way to the surface, often with uncomfortable results, and the more a national history is fossilized, the greater will be the discomfort. By its very nature, national history is teleological, and because it is teleological it is also reductionist. If the prime purpose of historical inquiry is considered to be the charting of a community's path towards self-realization as a nation, and ideally as one possessing all the apparatus of a sovereign state, important elements of its past are inevitably left out of account. Yet these elements can come back to haunt the present when the past is depicted in excessively simplistic terms.

During the nineteenth century and most of the twentieth the history of Europe, and by extension that of the European overseas world, was formulated in terms of the history of the construction and elaboration of the centralized nation state, which was seen as representing the culmination of a thousand years of European history. This conception of the European past was shaped on one hand by the reality of the establishment across the continent of regimes that succeeded in securing a degree of control over substantial areas of territory, and on the other by the stories that communities told about themselves as they sought to define their identities – stories that in due course tended to be appropriated by the state, or to coalesce around it. These stories existed long before the nineteenth century, but it was at the turn of the eighteenth and nineteenth centuries that the historical and philological inquiries associated with the Romantic movement gave them a new richness of texture that made possible the emergence of the sense of nationality which became so potent a feature of nineteenth- and twentieth-century European life.[16]

The effect of an approach coloured by a late eighteenth- and nineteenth-century vision of the nation has been to project onto earlier centuries interpretations of the past that do not necessarily accord with the political or cultural realities of the time. I found this in the course of my own researches into the response of seventeenth-century Catalans to the policies pursued by the government in Madrid. Catalonia presents a particularly interesting case study because of its importance in the Middle Ages as a dynamic member of the Crown of Aragon – the federation of the kingdoms of Aragon and Valencia and the Principality of Catalonia itself – and the driving force behind the construction of an Aragonese empire in the western Mediterranean. Medieval Catalonia, along with Valencia and Aragon, established an impressive set of representative institutions designed to ensure that the relationship between the prince and his people would be firmly grounded on a reciprocal contract. During the fifteenth century a Principality that had developed a rich commercial and cultural life lost some of its impetus as it succumbed to a prolonged period of civil and social conflict. When, following the marriage of Ferdinand and Isabella in 1469, it became no more than one among the several parts of a united 'Spain' (and subsequently of a worldwide Spanish Monarchy), it inevitably saw a diminution of its influence and importance in the world.

It is possible to imagine a set of historical circumstances as a result of which Catalonia might have become one of the centralized nation states of modern Europe like Portugal, its counterpart on the western fringes of the Iberian peninsula. History, however, moved in a different direction, and the Principality was relegated to the sidelines until it experienced a commercial and industrial revival in the eighteenth century. Consequently, Catalan historians have traditionally looked on the sixteenth and seventeenth centuries as a period of 'decadence', an unhappy interlude between a glorious past and a splendid future. That future, however, did not include its elevation to the ranks of Europe's sovereign nation states.

Questions have therefore arisen as to whether Catalonia in the centuries since the Union of the Crowns is to be seen as a nation state in embryo, an aborted nation state, or, as some Catalan historians now like to depict it, a nation state but with imperfect sovereignty. Similar questions were asked by Lucien Febvre of the Franche-Comté, another political and territorial entity that became one of the dominions of Charles V and his successors on the Spanish throne. Febvre's neglected classic *Philippe II et la Franche-Comté* (1912) made a deep impression on me, even deeper than that made by Braudel's *Méditerranée*, and provided a model that I sought to follow in my own work on Catalonia, since it seemed to me to succeed in reducing 'total history' to manageable proportions. What, asked Febvre, was the Franche-Comté – 'a province, part of a whole – or a little autonomous state?' His answer was double-edged. It was a province in the sense that it owed allegiance to a powerful sovereign who ruled over an agglomeration of German, Spanish, Italian and Flemish territories, of which it formed only one small and isolated part. But, as Febvre argued, it can also be classified as a state, albeit a small one, because of 'the autonomy it enjoyed, the liberties it retained, and the traditions it struggled to maintain. But this Comtois state was not sovereign; at decisive moments it received its orders from a distant master who necessarily had to subordinate to the interests of his general policy the particular interests of his Comtois domain.'[17] This was exactly the situation of Catalonia in the same period.

The ambiguity of Febvre's answers suggests that the criteria conventionally used by historians to determine the nature of statehood and the quality and quantity of national consciousness are those of modern times. While language, for instance, has always been an expression of group identity, it is not clear that it possessed the significance in earlier periods that it came to enjoy after Herder and the Romantics developed their organic concept of nation and *Volk*. Linguistic nationalism was often invented or promoted by nineteenth- and early twentieth-century intellectuals, some of them newcomers to the language which they now regarded as representing the authentic voice of the people.[18]

Where Catalonia is concerned, the vernacular was not only used for government and commerce during the Middle Ages, but also inspired a rich literary culture. In the sixteenth century, however, Catalan faced growing competition from other languages, and especially from Castilian, which, as the language of the court and the central administration of a worldwide empire, enjoyed obvious advantages over the other peninsular tongues. Although seventeenth-century Catalans were told, as I had been told in Barcelona, that they should be speaking the language of the empire, the defence of their native language, while a sensitive issue, did not possess priority in their long list of grievances. This is not entirely surprising, since Castilian held a growing appeal for the elite, even though Catalan continued to be the language of family and institutional life.[19] The eighteenth century saw further Castilian inroads, and it was only with the cultural renaissance of the nineteenth century that the Catalan language, with the encouragement of intellectuals who saw it as an essential mark of national identity, recovered its social standing and became once again the language of public discourse.[20]

Does the abandonment of its native language by an elite signify a decline of national consciousness, or is national consciousness itself in the early modern period of the sixteenth and seventeenth centuries a topic in need of serious rethinking? As I began to realize in the course of my researches, seventeenth-century Catalans talked a great deal about their *patria*. While the *patria* was, in the first instance, one's birthplace, home town or local region, the word also expressed the sense felt by Catalans of being members of a wider community. This community was defined by the *terra* – the beautiful and abundant land which they inhabited, by a shared history, by shared customs and characteristics, including law, language and religious fidelity, and by a common set of ideals. These ideals had enabled them to create what was, in their collective imagination, the perfect polity for a free people – a polity in which prince and people enjoyed a finely balanced reciprocal relationship based on mutual trust, and guaranteed by representative institutions through which the people could freely express their will. It was incumbent on each generation to preserve this polity, and transmit it intact to its successors.

In due course I came to appreciate that devotion to the *patria* was not confined to one society or region but was a common characteristic of early modern Europeans.[21] This devotion tends to be depicted as a kind of protonationalism, constituting no more than a staging-post on the road to the full-blooded nationalism of the nineteenth and twentieth centuries. While it certainly shared some of the traits of that nationalism, in that it was an expression of group identity to which memory and place, ethnicity and religion, were all likely to have contributed, it also possessed a legal and constitutional dimension largely absent today. Early modern societies thought instinctively in terms of law and precedent, and the *patria* of their collective imagining was an idealized polity endowed with an ancient constitution which was sanctified – although it might also be corrupted – by the passage of time.[22]

The notion of an ancient constitution was very much in the air at the time I was working on *The Revolt of the Catalans*, as a result of the publication in 1957 by John Pocock, another of Herbert Butterfield's research students, of his highly influential study of seventeenth-century English legal and historical thinking, *The Ancient Constitution and the Feudal Law*.[23]

Although I did not use the phrase 'ancient constitution' in my own book, Pocock's work certainly lay behind my comments on the way in which the Catalans saw their *patria* as a polity defined by its constitutional arrangements,[24] and reinforced my belief that early modern attitudes to the *patria* could only be fully understood if they took into account the importance of historical and legal thinking to the self-imagining of European societies in general.

As I came to see, the conceptualization of the *patria* in constitutional terms placed a powerful instrument in the hands of those opposed to what they saw as the arbitrary exercise of power. This was clear from the Catalan response in 1640 to the policies and actions of Madrid. But, as I was later to explain in 'Revolution and Continuity in Early Modern Europe', the inaugural lecture I gave in 1968 on taking up the chair of history at King's College, London, I thought that the community consciousness embodied in the concept of *patria* was a common and critical element in many of the major revolts that shook early modern Europe, including the revolt of the Netherlands in the 1560s against the government of Philip II and the English Revolution of the 1640s.[25]

Resistance based on the defence of an 'ancient constitution' inevitably conferred on early modern revolts an archaizing character which appeared to clash with conventional assumptions about the nature of revolts and revolutions at the time I was writing. I saw these early modern rebels as looking backwards rather than forwards, as they sought to reconstruct the idealized community of their imagining – a community now being threatened and subverted by the tyrannical actions of the prince and his ministers. Some of my Catalan critics were later to complain that my account depicted the rebels as reactionaries and Olivares and his ministerial colleagues in Madrid as the true representatives of modernity. But this was not my intention. Looking backwards does not automatically rule out moving forwards. The rebels against Philip II's government in the Netherlands may have been defending their traditional liberties as they looked back to the golden age of the Dukes of Burgundy, but the outcome of their struggle was the creation of a Dutch Republic which, while retaining numerous archaic constitutional arrangements, proved to be a pioneer in successfully confronting the new economic, religious and political challenges of the age. 'Modernity' has many faces, and the race is not always won by those who seem at the time to command the future.

It was partly to avoid such confusions that, like many other historians of my own and later generations, I came to embrace the notion of a distinctive 'early modern' period of European history, covering the centuries running from around the 1350s to the 1750s. The concept of an early modern period that was neither purely medieval nor purely modern but saw the coexistence of features regarded as characteristic of both epochs seems first to have been seriously advanced by economic historians in the 1930s.[26] As far as I am aware I first became conscious of the term and of its usefulness when G. N. Clark, himself an economic historian and, incidentally, one of the examiners of my doctoral thesis, published in 1954 a book entitled *The Early Modern Period* as the second volume of a three-volume history, *The European Inheritance*, that had its origins in a decision taken by a Conference of Allied Ministers of Education during the Second World War to assist in binding up the wounds of a war-torn Europe.[27]

Without giving the matter much thought, I came instinctively to see myself as an 'early modern' historian, but for a long time the term remained unfamiliar – so much so that when H. G. Koenigsberger and I approached the Cambridge University Press in the early 1960s with a proposal for a series entitled 'Cambridge Studies in Early Modern History', it was turned down on the grounds that nobody knew what 'early modern' meant. But when we tried again, in 1966, our suggestion was accepted, and a series was launched that would survive until the end of the twentieth century and would do much, with almost fifty titles to its credit, to establish the notion of a distinctive 'early modern' period.

The volumes carried an introductory note to the effect that the idea of an 'early modern' period of European history extending from the fifteenth to the late eighteenth century was now finding wide acceptance among historians. It said that the purpose of the series was to publish studies that would help to illustrate the character of the period as a whole, and in particular 'to focus attention on dominant themes within it – the interplay of continuity (the continuity of medieval ideas, and forms of political and social organization) and change (the impact of new ideas, new methods and new demands on the traditional structures)'.

All attempts at historical periodization are by nature unsatisfactory because no single term can hope to encapsulate the character of an epoch as a whole. 'Early modern' is similarly inadequate, and runs the risk of suggesting that the period is no more than a staging-post on the road to contemporary society. But no better term has yet been found for a period of three to four centuries in which the medieval and the 'modern' interact in fascinating combination. The unwillingness to recognize the distinctiveness of these pre-Enlightenment centuries has tended to vitiate our understanding of important features of European society of the time, and in no field of historical study is this truer than in that of nationalism and state development.

If, as I believe, the viewing of societies before the age of the French Revolution through the lens of nineteenth- and twentieth-century nationalism introduces distorting effects, the same is true of the attempt to view them through the lens of the modern centralized state. Europe before the age of the French Revolution was made up of a wide variety of polities of different shapes and sizes, including small city-states and medium-sized republics like Switzerland and Venice, principalities, duchies, kingdoms and large-scale composite states, some of which could lay claim to the status of empires. During the sixteenth century the Roman law maxim that 'a king is emperor in his own kingdom' evolved, in the hands of Jean Bodin, into a fully articulated theory of sovereignty, and the doctrine of inalienable and indivisible sovereignty became a potent weapon in the hands of princes as they sought to define their position in relation to their own subjects and to other princes.

Such assertions of sovereignty could be used to facilitate the concentration of power in the hands of the prince and his administration, in a process that later ages would describe as 'state building' or 'centralization' – the concept that originally attracted me to the career and policies of Olivares as a subject for research. Neither expression satisfactorily expresses the complex processes under way across much of early modern Europe. There is now a greater realization of the continuing strength of dynasticism in the early modern period than there was at the time I began my researches. In European societies that were built around the family unit, princes thought instinctively in terms of family and dynasty, and pursued strategies – as did their subjects – which were designed to consolidate and extend the family's power and influence. It was the matrimonial politics of the great ruling houses of Europe, the Habsburgs, the Trastámaras and the Tudors, along with the series of dynastic accidents that were the inevitable accompaniment of those strategies, which brought about the union of distinct and sometimes very different polities under a single ruler, and led to the formation of large supranational political and administrative groupings like that ruled by the Emperor Charles V or the one governed by his son and heir, Philip II of Spain.

These larger political groupings have come to be known in recent years as 'composite monarchies' or 'composite states', a term that was not in use at the time I was working on *The Revolt of the Catalans*, and that seems to have been invented in the mid-1970s by my successor at King's College, London,

Professor H. G. Koenigsberger.[28] If I did not employ the term, however, I was very well aware of the reality behind it, since Catalonia, like the many other provinces and kingdoms which formed part of the vast supranational structure of the Spanish Monarchy, was daily faced with the implications of being ruled from a distance by a monarch who counted numerous other peoples among his subjects.

The most obvious of those implications to contemporaries was more or less permanent royal absenteeism. Royal absenteeism and the difficulties of adjusting to it were central to my reading of the problems of early seventeenth-century Catalonia. It is true that the absence of their prince was not exactly a novelty to the Catalans, who had experienced long periods of royal absence in the age of the medieval Catalan–Aragonese federation. But he was now in Madrid, surrounded by Castilians, and the policies he pursued appeared to bear little or no relation to the interests of his Catalan subjects. Since the prince formed an integral part of the idealized *patria*, it was not easy for seventeenth-century Catalans, any more than it had been for the sixteenth-century inhabitants of the Netherlands, to come to terms with the notion of conflict rather than cooperation between prince and people. A central theme of my book was the breakdown of the traditional perception of the *patria* as an organic union of prince and people, as loyalties were placed under growing strain and choices were imposed where ideally none should have been necessary, or capable of even being contemplated. In 1640 prince *and patria* gave way to prince *or patria*, and the outcome was revolt.

Similar stories were repeated across Europe during the middle decades of the seventeenth century in a series of contemporaneous revolts and revolutions that shook the European monarchies. The character and causes of these revolts and revolutions became the subject of impassioned historical debate in the 1950s and 1960s, following the publication in 1954, in the historical journal *Past and Present*, of an article by one of Britain's leading Marxist historians, Eric Hobsbawm, on 'The General Crisis of the European Economy in the Seventeenth Century'. Hobsbawm's prime concern was the timing of the transition from feudalism to capitalism, and he depicted the seventeenth century as an age of crisis for the European economy – a crisis that was to provide the impetus for social revolt in the middle decades of the century.

Much of the resulting debate on what came to be known as 'The General Crisis of the Seventeenth Century' was conducted in the pages of *Past and Present*, whose editorial board I was invited to join in 1958 as part of an attempt to free it of its overly Marxist associations, which had become an impediment to its growth and circulation in the ideologically divided world of the Cold War era (Plate 5). It was a debate that involved many of the most prominent British, European and American historians of the day. Although, like most historical debates, it gradually petered out as historians grew weary of grazing increasingly well-worn fields and moved on in search of fresher pastures, it did much to stimulate thought about the nature of European society and the European state in the early modern period. Now, in the opening years of the twenty-first century, it shows signs of springing into life once again.[29]

The persistence of the debate provides some indication of the richness of the subject and the significance of the points at issue to more than one generation of historians. Viewed in retrospect the General Crisis controversy marks a critical moment in the history of twentieth-century historical writing. The economic and social interpretation of the past was dominant in the post-Second World War period, and even the anti-Marxist Hugh Trevor-Roper, who responded to Hobsbawm's article in the most scintillating of the many contributions to the debate, constructed his reply within the same frame of reference. In the spirit of the age, he sought to explain the 'Puritan Revolution' and the other contemporaneous revolts in terms of underlying social and economic developments, although placing his own original spin on the discussion by postulating, both for England and for the continent, a sharp divide between 'court' and 'country' – a divide that he explained with characteristic ingenuity.[30]

My own reading of the Catalan revolt made me sceptical of interpretations of revolution which, in imitation of the prevailing model of the causes of the French Revolution, found the key in long-term economic and social trends. I was more struck by the pressures emanating from above, in the form of initiatives taken by the prince and his state apparatus, than by the pressures from below. It seemed to me that these initiatives were generated in particular by international rivalries and the demands of war, and other contributors to the debate adopted a similar line. Although this alternative explanation in no way ruled out the impact of economic and social forces on the course of events, it did suggest the need to see the state as an agent in its own right, responding to its own imperatives and pursuing its own distinctive agenda, on which considerations of dynastic interest and royal prestige ranked high.

Since the years when the General Crisis debate was at its height, and perhaps in part as a consequence of that debate, historians have shown a renewed interest in the character, the structure and the operations of the state as an agent of change. This might be regarded as the overdue reinsertion of politics into history, after a long period of its relegation to the sidelines at a time when economic and social interpretations were in the ascendant. The rediscovery of the state, however, is something more than a return to old ways of thinking. A newer generation of historians has come to look at the state in less purely institutional terms than was common among their nineteenth- and early twentieth-century predecessors, the narrowness of whose approach provoked the *Annales* counter-revolution led by Marc Bloch, Lucien Febvre and Fernand Braudel. In recent years the study of the state and of state-formation has expanded to include such topics as political culture, the nature of kingship and royal courts, and the working of patronage and clientage systems.[31]

The whole notion of 'state-building', however, has tended to vitiate our approach to the critical early modern period of the fifteenth to eighteenth centuries. While the 'state' and state power figured with increasing prominence in the political discourse of the period, the forms of political organization did not necessarily move by an ineluctable progression in one single direction. If princes sought to strengthen their power by extending the reach of their officials to outlying regions and provinces, they all too often found their attempts frustrated by the resistance of their subjects.

This resistance frequently assumed an institutionalized form in the activities of parliaments and Estates. The study of these has had a long history, particularly in the Anglo-American world, whose historians have traditionally paid close attention to parliamentary origins and the history of political represen-tation as a consequence of the centrality of representative institutions to British and American life. But the great German historian Otto Hintze (1861–1940), who was much concerned with the history of state-formation, possessed an equal interest in the history of constitutionalism and published in 1931 an influential essay in comparative and global history reviewing the origins of representative government.[32] Five years later the International Commission for the History of Representative and Parliamentary Institutions was established, but 1936 was hardly the most propitious of moments for an initiative of this kind, and it was only with the revival of democratic institutions across western Europe in the post-war period that the study of parliaments and Estates became a serious international enter-prise. The result was a steady flow of monographs, of which one of the most suggestive and wide-ranging was the state-by-state study *Princes and Parliaments in Germany* by a German Jewish refugee to Britain, Francis Carsten (1911–98), who showed how, with the significant exception of Bavaria, the normal expectation in sixteenth-century German states was of cooperation rather than conflict between ruler and Estates. Jean Bodin expressed the conventional sixteenth-century view of the underlying harmony of this relationship when he wrote, 'The majesty of the prince is most fully manifested in the assembly of the three estates of the whole realm.'[33]

A series of problems, of which one of the most acute was the emergence of differences of religion between ruler and subject in the age of the Reformation and Counter-Reformation, placed growing strains on the relationship, and over many parts of Europe the nominally harmonious partnership collapsed in the revolts and revolutions of the middle decades of the seventeenth century. As I tried to show in *The Revolt of the Catalans*, the composite nature of the Spanish Monarchy and the royal absenteeism that was its natural consequence contributed significantly to the breakdown of relations in the seventeenth-century Iberian peninsula.

Just as I drew inspiration for these ideas from Febvre's study of Philip II and the Franche-Comté, so Conrad Russell drew inspiration from my study of Philip IV and Catalonia for his own work on the difficulties of Charles I and the origins of the English Civil War. 'The hypothesis that the problem of multiple kingdoms was a major cause of instability in Britain', he wrote, 'looks perfectly plausible when considered in a European context.'[34] Such mutual influences provide an illustration of the continuity of the historical enterprise over the generations, and of the way in which seeds, once sown, may lie dormant for a while before sprouting or, alternatively, by being carried in the air, can spring to life in unexpected places. From the Franche-Comté to the British Isles by way of Catalonia is not the most obvious of trajectories.

Religion was one potential cause of conflict between prince and people. Fiscalism was another. Taxation was heavy and growing heavier, in part because of the costs of Trevor-Roper's 'court', which he extended to include the bureaucratic apparatus of royal officials, but more especially because of the escalating costs of European warfare caused by important tactical and technological changes – the famous 'Military Revolution' of the British historian of Sweden Michael Roberts, who launched the concept in an inaugural lecture in 1955.[35] The need to mobilize the human and material resources of the states they governed in order to wage and sustain their wars in an age of almost continuous warfare drove rulers to engage in all manner of financial expedients and extortions, which inevitably bore down most heavily on those least able to bear them. It also impelled them to find ways of galvanizing their sluggish bureaucracies, and of short-circuiting traditional procedures by appointing new officials, like the French *intendants*, drawn from outside the ranks of those who belonged to traditional office-holding dynasties. In the process they resorted to every kind of device that would enhance their own authority, and found a pretext for their authoritarian behaviour in arguments drawn from 'reason of state' and the doctrine that necessity knew no law.

This new authoritarianism, which was less the product of conscious 'state-building' than of the imperatives of the moment arising in large part from the exigencies of war, led rulers to ride roughshod over traditional laws, practices and constitutional rights. Inevitably this set them on a collision course with representative institutions and with large sections of the population, who saw themselves subjected to the arbitrary exercise of power and found their traditional liberties under attack. In outlying regions, and especially in composite monarchies where different kingdoms and provinces retained their semi-autonomous status, it proved difficult, if not impossible, to enforce the royal will in the face of such resistance. In extreme cases – in the British Isles, the Iberian peninsula, Spanish Italy and the France of Richelieu and Mazarin – the outcome was revolt.

Yet some areas flared up in revolt while others remained quiescent. Why should this have been? Historians are accustomed to searching for the causes of revolution, but have spent considerably less time looking for those of non-revolution. Like Sherlock Holmes's dog that did not bark in the night, however, this too can tell us something. In particular, it can throw light on the forces, or the practices, that made for stability in the inherently unstable societies of early modern Europe, and so, by extension, draw attention to their possible absence or weakness in those societies that flared up in revolt. Catalonia's neighbour, the kingdom of Valencia, found itself under comparable pressure as a result of Madrid's attempts in the 1620s and 1630s to mobilize its resources for war. The Valencians were as devoted to their *patria* as the Catalans, but, unlike the Catalans, they did not rebel. How is the difference to be explained?

This was the historical conundrum that a former student of mine, James Casey, set out to solve in a doctoral thesis written in the 1960s. Himself coming from a peripheral province, Northern Ireland, at the moment when it was descending into its time of troubles, he was naturally attracted by the prospect of studying the reasons for non-revolution in another peripheral province, Valencia, at a potentially revolutionary moment. In the book that eventually emerged from his researches, *The Kingdom of Valencia in the Seventeenth Century*, he identified a number of possible reasons for the relative quiescence of Valencian society in the age of Olivares, but one in particular stood out. Everywhere he found what he called 'threads of personal dependence' running across the divide, and preventing 'the development of any clean split between governors and governed'.[36]

Over the past two or three decades historians of early modern Europe have devoted much attention to these 'threads of personal dependence' operating through kinship networks and patron–client relationships.[37] Running from top to bottom of corporate and hierarchically organized societies, these relationships might provoke faction feuds and divisions, but they also endowed those societies with a vertical articulation that, if skilfully manipulated, could bind court and country together in a reciprocal relationship. In particular they could do much to secure and maintain political stability by binding the court nobility and provincial and local elites to the crown in a system of mutual dependence, under which the monarch dispensed rewards in return for real or alleged services. An important part of these services was to provide government at the local level in the absence of a professional civil service large enough, and reliable enough, to execute royal commands.

The effect was to create a system of negotiated government that maintained a degree of law and order across the continent during the early modern centuries, although with periodic breakdowns in certain places, as in the middle decades of the seventeenth century. The prominence given in recent historical literature to the process of negotiation has dispelled the conventional image of this period as that of an 'age of absolutism', in which princes imposed power from the centre. Instead, we now have a more subtle picture of royal government as a transactional arrangement, in which the different parties manoeuvred and sought to apply various kinds of pressure in the expectation of striking an eventual bargain. This would seem to hold as true for the France of that allegedly quintessential 'absolutist' Louis XIV as for the Valencia of his uncle Philip IV of Spain.[38] Yet there are dangers, which have not entirely been avoided, in this new interpretation. It is easy to forget that monarchs, at least potentially, had resources at their disposal which far exceeded those at the disposal of even their greatest subjects. Not for nothing was the seventeenth century the age of Hobbes's *Leviathan*. Behind the power of the word lay the power of the sword.

The preamble to a French royal decree of 1599 prohibiting duels stated that 'le roi seul a droit de glaive' – the king alone has the right of the sword.[39] While for a long time this might have been little more than an aspiration, the increasing complexity and cost of warfare in a continent almost permanently at war had conspired to make it a reality over much of western and central Europe by the end of the seventeenth century. Following the mid-century upheavals, and partly in response to them, more power was being concentrated in the hands of central governments, and a combination of fear and self-interest, along with the progressive domestication of previously unruly elites, was ushering in a new age of at least relative stability.[40]

The stability, however, was more obvious on the domestic scene than in the arena of international relations where, as ever, prince confronted prince, and state confronted state. The effect of international rivalries over the sixteenth and seventeenth centuries was to sharpen national sentiment, at least where princes managed to rally popular support for their wars. As the hostility between the England of Elizabeth I and the Spain of Philip II vividly reveals, the sense of national and collective identity was reinforced by the development of religious hatreds in a continent polarized from the mid-sixteenth century onwards between Protestants and Catholics. This was the continent whose fortunes I sought to chart in *Europe Divided, 1559–1598*, a book commissioned in the 1960s for a highly successful series of volumes covering relatively short chrono-logical periods of European history from the later Middle Ages onwards.[41] My brief was to bring some coherence to the history of an extremely complex period characterized by bitter religious conflicts, rebellion and civil wars in a Europe over-shadowed by the looming presence of a Spain that was widely thought to be on the road to universal monarchy.

It was in the seventeenth century, according to G. N. Clark, that 'historians began to treat the history of Europe in the way that is still common, as an aggregate of the histories of different countries'.[42] This was certainly the convention in the mid-twentieth century: my own lecture course on European history between 1500 and 1700 in the Cambridge of the 1950s and 1960s was largely constructed along national and regional lines. But in addressing the problem of providing a comprehensible account of a continent in turmoil during the later sixteenth century I became increasingly aware of the inadequacy of this approach. I realized that it was essential to cut across national boundaries, just as competing religions cut across them in the sixteenth century, transcending national loyalties by requiring a superior loyalty to an international faith. Only by following the interaction of people, ideas and events across the continent was it possible to bring home to readers the importance for contemporaries of the issues at stake, capture something of the excitement and unpredictability of the times, and suggest why developments turned out as they did.

In effect I was writing what has recently come to be known as 'transnational history'. This, as I see it, is much more than the conventional history of international relations, dependent on diplomatic narrative and that chronicling of mere 'events' so despised by Braudel. It also involves the discussion of international contacts at every level, and of the mutual influence and interplay of beliefs, values, cultural attitudes and political programmes between two or more societies. This charting of a process of continuous interaction is likely to bring us closer to the realities of a Europe that was politically and religiously divided while possessing common cultural traits than the historical discussion of domestic developments as if states were hermetically sealed off from contact with their neighbours. Whether they chose to imitate or reject the model placed before them by their European rivals, monarchs and ministers were continuously watching, and learning from, each other.[43]

The seventeenth century saw the development of two distinct models of political organization. One was fashioned by the Dutch Republic, which astonished contemporaries by showing that a republican or near-republican society with strong representative institutions and a diversity of faiths could not only survive but prosper in a highly competitive world. Against this Dutch model, or Anglo-Dutch model as it became as the century drew to a close, was ranged a French model shaped by more or less authoritarian kingship and uniformity of religion. The contrast between the two models is vividly reflected in the divergent trajectories taken by two composite monarchies, the Spanish and the British, in the opening years of the eighteenth century. The Anglo-Scottish union of 1707 created a parliamentary-style composite monarchy, with Scotland retaining its own church and laws but participating in the Westminster parliament of a United Kingdom. By contrast, between 1709 and 1716 the new Bourbon dynasty established on the Spanish throne following the War of the Spanish Succession abolished the traditional liberties and representative institutions of Aragon, Catalonia and Valencia, making their systems of government uniform with the more authoritarian system that prevailed in Castile.[44] In the same period, the Viennese Habsburgs would try but fail to reduce the kingdom of Hungary to uniformity with their other territories, their failure paving the way for the Dual Monarchy of the nineteenth century.[45]

The events of the late seventeenth and the eighteenth centuries would show that, of the two competing models of state organization, the Anglo-Dutch model possessed greater resilience and staying-power than the French or Spanish, even in that area where authoritarianism would seem at first sight to enjoy the advantage – the waging of war. Liberty and representative institutions proved in the long run to offer a better recipe for raising revenues and ensuring credit-worthiness than government decrees and royal promises.[46]

Over much of eighteenth-century Europe, governments, irrespective of whether they were authoritarian or libertarian in character, succeeded in strengthening their corps of professional administrators, securing a firmer hold over their populations and raising men and money for their wars more effectively than in earlier times. While the old Europe of corporate rights and privileges persisted and flourished,[47] the power of the state was manifestly growing, and rulers presented themselves as the embodiment of that power. But although by this time it is possible to speak of European 'states' and a European 'state system', those states still retained the characteristics of the traditional social order, which indeed displayed a remarkable resilience right up to the period of the First World War.[48]

Dynastic interests continued to weigh heavily on the formulation of policy, and kingdoms and provinces were exchanged between rulers without regard for the feelings of their inhabitants, as if they were no more than family properties to be disposed of at will. The continent remained what it had been for centuries – a patchwork of polities, running all the way from prince-bishoprics to large composite monarchies.

It would take the French Revolution and the Napoleonic Wars to shake this traditional Europe to its foundations. Subjects were transformed into citizens, and, all the way from Spain to Russia, the continent witnessed an upsurge of national sentiment of an intensity hitherto unknown. As nineteenth-century governments succeeded in harnessing this sentiment and appropriating it to themselves, the centralized or centralizing nation state became a political reality. Yet, even now, it failed to sweep everything before it. The composite monarchy known as the Austro-Hungarian Empire would survive until 1918. It would take the Versailles settlement and the doctrine of national self-determination to transform Europe into a continent of sovereign nation states. But the redrawing of the map would leave behind it a trail of suppressed nationalities – those peoples who found themselves on the wrong side of history when the music was abruptly stopped in 1918–19, and, for one reason or another, were excluded when the prizes were distributed.

It is not surprising that, in the century or century and a half when nation states established themselves as the dominant form of political organization, historians should have devoted themselves in such numbers to the writing of national histories, which all too often became an exaltation of the state. A new age, however, brings new perspectives and new priorities. The nation state, while remaining the standard form of political organization, has been under growing pressure both from above and from below since the end of the Second World War. From above, it has been compelled to yield ground to international and supranational bodies, of which the European Community is a prime example. From below, it has come under pressure from the 'suppressed nationalities', and from regions and ethnicities demanding their own place in the sun. As a result, what once seemed certain has become less certain, and structures that once had about them an air of permanence are showing signs of frailty.

It is only to be expected that these changes should be reflected in current historical writing. The move in recent years to global history, transcending that of nations and states, is one indication of the changing times.[49] So, too, is the interest in forms of political organization that crossed national boundaries, like the composite empire of Charles V, too easily perceived as a harbinger of European unity.[50] If the reconciliation of unity with diversity has shown itself to be a central challenge of our age, historians have understandably turned their attention to earlier efforts to address the same problem. The tension between the vision of a united Europe and the particularism of the parts into which it is divided has been a constant of European history from Roman times to our own.

Similarly, as the centralized nation state has also come under pressure from below, it is not surprising that historians in recent years should have challenged and attacked the received narrative that, for the past century or more, has been taught to its citizens. It is no accident that Great Britain in the age of devolution and the new Spain of the autonomous communities should both have seen vigorous challenges to the standard accounts of their national pasts. In both countries the dominant partner in the union of realms shaped and controlled the traditional narrative: British history was treated as essentially English history, while Spanish history was subsumed under the history of Castile. Over the past few decades both these standard narratives have been subjected to a process of deconstruction. What was once primarily English history has become the history of the British Isles – or even, in one formulation, simply of 'the Isles'[51] – while the history of Spain has been broken down into that of its different regions.

This process of historical deconstruction has had a salutary effect in forcing the creative rethinking of so-called 'national' histories that privileged the dominant part of the nation state at the expense of the others. Yet it is also in danger of generating a no less distorted picture of the past. Political fragmentation carries within it the virus of historical fragmentation. Already a new generation in eastern Spain is in danger of reaching maturity under the impression that the history of its native territory stops at the banks of the river Ebro. Such an approach inevitably leads back to the enclosed and narrow nationalist history that historians of the stature of Vicens Vives made it their mission to undermine.

For good or ill, during centuries of union with a more powerful neighbour, Catalonia, Valencia and the Basque Provinces, like Scotland, Wales and Ireland, have formed part of a state, more or less composite in character, whose history they shared. The slate cannot be wiped clean by removing this perhaps inconvenient historical fact from the record and rewriting the history of the individual regions or communities as if it had never occurred. The interplay between the various parts of that state is in itself a revealing story, raising significant questions about what was lost or gained by union, and shedding light on what differentiated its component parts and on what they had in common. This is also a story in continuous process of evolution, and nobody can know how it will end. But as our own generation, like its predecessors, seeks to reconcile the conflicting claims of unity and diversity, historians can make their own contribution by reminding their readers of the complexity of all historical developments, and by pointing to the paths not taken, or forgotten. It is not beyond the bounds of possibility that the history of the Austro-Hungarian Empire or of Spain's composite monarchy under the House of Austria, both of them relegated by historians of the nation state to the dust-heap of history, might still have something to say to a very different age.

CHAPTER THREE

Political history and biography

My long years of work on the Catalan revolt of 1640 led me down unexpected avenues of historical inquiry, and gave me a set of insights into the nature of Spanish and also European history that might otherwise have eluded me. They introduced me to the fraught question of nationality and collective identity, and forced me to grapple with issues in political, cultural and economic history that gave me a better understanding of the societies of early modern Europe and of the tensions that could drive them down the road to revolution. Yet even as research, writing and the teaching of undergraduate and graduate students widened my horizons and helped give me a sense of the interconnected nature of past and present, I still had a gnawing feeling of unfinished business. The Prado's portrait of Olivares refused to let me go.

Why do historians feel drawn to study particular periods and personalities rather than others? As far as my own engagement with the Count-Duke was concerned, it was in the first instance the sheer grandeur of Velázquez's masterful portrait that attracted my interest. Was it also something about the arrogance of power so nakedly displayed that aroused my curiosity, although not my sympathy? Whatever one's reaction, this is not a figure who can be ignored. Yet in the historical literature a man who ruled Spain and bestrode the European political stage for twenty-two years had received extraordinarily little attention, whether viewed from the standpoint of his contemporary importance, or measured against the enormous degree of interest generated by the figure of his more successful rival, Cardinal Richelieu. There was a gap here that somehow needed to be filled, and in studying one aspect of his domestic policies – his relations with the Catalans – I had at least taken a first step in repairing what increasingly appeared to me a serious historical oversight. But was there any possibility of carrying my interest any further?

The destruction by fire of the Count-Duke's personal archive in the late eighteenth century seemed to rule out the kind of intense study of the man and his policies that Richelieu had received.[1] Eight volumes of the Cardinal's correspondence and state papers were published by Avenel between 1853 and 1877, and the six-volume biography by Gabriel Hanotaux and the Duc de La Force was only the largest of the numerous treatments of Richelieu's life and career available in print.[2] By contrast, apart from the psychological biography by Gregorio

Marañón,[3] and some interesting attempts at an assessment of his policies by the nineteenth-century Spanish statesman Antonio Cánovas del Castillo,[4] there was a notable absence of work on Olivares, and hardly any of his state papers had seen the light of day.

The need for more work seemed obvious, but I had doubts about its feasibility. My study of Madrid's policies towards the Catalans had, however, yielded a substantial number of *consultas* or reports of discussions in the Spanish Council of State and other councils and juntas, in which the Count-Duke expressed his views, often at great length. While the *consultas* of the Council of State were overwhelmingly concerned with questions relating to foreign affairs – relations with France, England, the Holy Roman Empire and the Italian states – their survival in massive quantities for the 1620s and 1630s would at least make it possible to examine in considerable detail the intentions and activities of Olivares as a European statesman. This might be some way from my original ambition of studying his programme for domestic reform and regeneration, but there was obviously a close and continuing interaction between his foreign and domestic policies. Foreign policy decisions involving peace and war inevitably had a direct impact on internal developments in the Iberian peninsula, while dramatic internal developments, like the Catalan and Portuguese rebellions of 1640, had profound consequences for Spain's standing as the dominant power in Europe. Since the Count-Duke was prone at the least excuse to expatiate at length on the latest piece of news from across the continent, examining it from all angles and setting it into the broad context of the crown's international standing and the resources at its disposal, the study of his interventions in the Council of State, along with the various position papers he liked to dictate, provided a potentially rich source for the reconstruction of his political career.

There was, too, the possibility of supplementing this documentation, largely housed in the archive of Simancas, with documents from other public and also private archives, both in Spain and further afield. But the identification and investigation of these archives was likely to be a demanding and time-consuming business, and while in post, first in Cambridge and then, from 1968 to 1973, at King's College, London, my teaching and other duties allowed me only a very limited amount of time for concentrated archival research. With no documentation online, as it is in massive quantities today, there was no alternative other than to go in person to an archive or make a request for photocopies which might, or might not, be granted.

In 1973, however, I was fortunate enough to be appointed to a permanent position on the Faculty of the Institute for Advanced Study in Princeton. The purpose of the Institute as outlined at the time of its foundation in 1930 was to enable scholars to pursue their chosen line of inquiry in ways that would allow them to realize their full potential without the normal teaching and administrative commitments of academic life. Although I had learnt an enormous amount both from my undergraduate teaching and from exchanging ideas with my graduate students, who formed a glittering group in the

Cambridge of the 1960s, I realized that the move to Princeton would enable me to undertake the large-scale project that had been in my mind since the start of my career as a historian – the study of seventeenth-century Spain and the ministry of Olivares. This was an opportunity not to be missed.

My new-found freedom made it possible for me to comb the archives of Spain, Italy and other parts of Europe in search of the Count-Duke's letters and papers, and the despatches of diplomats reporting home from the court in Madrid. In the course of my wanderings I hit on some fascinating material, including important exchanges of correspondence between Olivares and Spanish envoys and officials in Flanders and elsewhere. There was enough of this documentation to suggest that, even if the Count-Duke's own archive, containing the bulk of his papers on the government of Spain, was irretrievably gone, it might nevertheless be possible to write what I envisaged from the beginning as being a political biography, although one that was bound to be slanted by the bias of the documents towards his conduct of foreign as distinct from domestic policy.

Yet before I could embark on writing it became obvious that it would be necessary to analyse closely the documents I had collected, and to collate those that had survived in a number of copies. In Spain there has been no strong tradition among historians of publishing documents in annotated editions, and although important documentary series exist, little or no attempt was made by their editors to discuss their provenance, collate the variations, and set the documents into their historical context. At this point my training as a Cambridge undergraduate in reading and commenting on the documents of English constitutional history came into its own. The same techniques could be applied to Olivares's letters and state papers as British historians were accustomed to applying to the papers and correspondence of monarchs and ministers. A volume, or volumes, containing a selection of documents running from the beginning to the end of Olivares's tenure of power would both serve my own immediate purposes and provide a useful tool for future historians of the period.

When I started, however, I had not quite appreciated the magnitude and complexity of the undertaking. The documents had to be deciphered, transcribed and collated, and numerous references to people, places and events tracked down. Here I was fortunate to have the help of a young historian from Andalusia, José Francisco de la Peña, who had been virtually brought up in the archives of Seville, where his father had been director of the Archive of the Indies. As my research assistant in Princeton over a period of five years he provided the linguistic knowledge and detective skills that are essential for textual work of this kind. Even then, however, the work of editing proved very demanding. Spain had nothing comparable to the *Dictionary of National Biography* or similar compilations for other leading European states, and we found ourselves having to ferret out biographical details even of major personalities who had received little or no attention in the historical literature. With the period seriously understudied, every document became a kind of obstacle course, as we sought to unravel its obscurities, elucidate its allusions, and introduce it with a short essay that would place it in its historical context.

As far as my own biographical project was concerned, the two volumes that emerged from this time-consuming but absorbing labour served as an indispensable ground-clearing operation.[5] The work of editing and annotating took me into areas that I might otherwise have neglected to explore, and forced me to grapple with problems that I might otherwise have side-stepped. Above all, it made me appreciate the importance of close textual study as the essential basis for any wide-ranging historical enterprise. At the same time, however, I also came to appreciate how dangerously all-absorbing editorial work can be. The tracking down of an obscure reference and the consequent resolution of even the most minor of editorial questions can be a source of such intense satisfaction that the excitement of the chase is liable to become an end in itself. All too easily, editing can transform itself into mere antiquarianism, and, as Dr Johnson asserted, 'a mere antiquarian is a rugged being'.

Yet there is no activity equal to editing as a means of immersing oneself in an age, and total immersion is essential if it is to be brought to life. There is more to historical writing, however, than evocation, important as this is. My principal interest was in grappling with some of the questions that have long exercised historians of Spain but that also have a more general resonance. One of the foremost of these questions was that of its 'decline'. Essentially this was the question of how and why the dominant European power lost its position in the middle decades of the seventeenth century and began to fall behind its north European rivals in a number of spheres of activity – economic, intellectual, scientific and technological. I therefore had to ask myself whether biography was the best way, or even a good way, of approaching what I saw as being the central issue of this period of the Spanish past.

The trend of the times was against me, at least in the context of the most recent developments in European historical writing. Although the biographical tradition remained strong in Britain, the *Annales* school had little time or use for biographies.[6] Over European historiography in the 1940s and 1950s loomed the shadow of Braudel, and he had made his views crystal clear. 'When I think of the individual,' he wrote in his *Méditerranée*, 'I am always inclined to see him imprisoned within a destiny in which he himself has little hand.'[7] Although Braudel was never a full-blown economic or geographical determinist, and was prepared to concede that one or two strong personalities might on occasion prove capable of wrenching open a bar on the prison window, he believed that the constraints imposed by unyielding economic realities and the iron laws of the environment made actual escape virtually impossible.[8] While Braudel himself was capable of producing brilliant pen portraits of such figures as Philip II, their subjects were no more than incidental to the exposition of the great and often glacial processes underlying human history.

I had already ignored Braudel's advice in pressing on with my research into Olivares's attempts at reform, and I was well aware of his doubts about biography as a contribution to historical writing. Indeed, he had appeared in print on the subject, and specifically in relation to Olivares and one or two of his contemporaries, in 1947, two years before the publication of his *Méditerranée*. The occasion was a review of three books, one of which was Dr Marañón's psychoanalytical biography of the Count-Duke, which, although first published in 1936, had just appeared in a German translation.[9] While describing Marañon's book as 'brilliant', he criticized the author for setting the personality he had so skilfully dissected against the picture of an age that, as depicted by Marañón, was 'no more than a summary background, a theatre backcloth, rather than being what it is: a source of life'. After going on to condemn in general the 'impenitent writers of biographies' for pouring out a stream of portraits with 'false perspectives and conventional designs', he conceded, perhaps surprisingly in view of his generally low view of *histoire biographique*, that 'biography is the most difficult genre of historical writing: at every instant the personality escapes historians, snaps his fingers at us, or, when he abandons himself to us, leaves in our hands no more than a skin that is not always his'. He ended his disheartening observations on the difficulties and failings of biographers with the following throwaway lines: 'I must confess that, if I had the desire to study the Count-Duke of Olivares, I should recoil before the immensity of the task. Is it possible to capture the man if one does not follow his labours day by day over more than twenty years – a man who was the master of the Hispanic empire, and who was incessantly reading, writing, and issuing orders in his attempt to thwart or exploit circumstances as they arose? And, even after such an investigation, what do we know of the man?' These were not words designed to encourage a potential biographer of the Count-Duke.

While I was perfectly willing to follow Olivares's labours 'day by day over more than twenty years' if the documentation allowed me to do so, I had to think hard about whether the exercise was worth the effort, and what it was that I really wanted it to achieve. Was this to be yet another biography of a leading European statesman? Here I was at once hindered and helped by the existence of Marañón's impressive book, which was based on extensive reading in a range of seventeenth-century sources. The conventional aspects of a biography – an examination of the subject's background, personality, lifestyle and relationships – had already been covered by Marañón, even if not in a conventional way. The result was a remarkable book, even though Braudel had correctly pointed to its principal weakness – its failure to explore in any depth the relationship of its central figure to the social, political and cultural environment in which, as a politician, he was compelled to operate.

Marañón's biography of the Count-Duke, with its illuminating subtitle 'La pasión de mandar' – the passion to command – was very much a product of its age, even if he approached his task in a highly distinctive way. Historical biography enjoyed enormous popularity in the 1920s and 1930s, and especially biography informed by psychoanalysis. Marañón knew Freud's work well and recognized its great importance, but he harboured doubts about certain aspects of it, and seems to have felt that it tended to universalize psychological traits that might be peculiar to central Europe and were not necessarily to be found in other cultural areas.[10] He was more directly influenced by the work of Ernst Kretschmer, a professor at the University of Marburg, and a leading figure in the movement in 1920s' Germany to extend the range of psychiatry to include the human physique. Marañón, who was effectively the founder of Spanish endocrinology, was much influenced by Kretschmer's theories about the close relationship between personality and physique, and although he never succumbed to a crude biological determinism, he sought to classify the subjects of his historical biographies, including Olivares, in conformity with Kretschmer's 'biotypes'.[11]

Kretschmer's classifications have not stood the test of time, but they enabled Marañón to paint a vivid portrait of the short, stocky and obese Count-Duke as a 'pyknic' type with a cycloid temperament, as compared with his rival, Richelieu, classified as an 'asthenic' type with a schizoid temperament. Olivares, as depicted by Marañon, conformed to the traits of the pyknic in his sharp alternations of mood between elation and depression. In moments of elation he would be swept onwards by his optimism, engaging in grand projects with boundless energy, and displaying an infinite capacity for hard work. Then he would sink into a profound depression, experiencing a period of spiritual and physical collapse, only to emerge with renewed energies until the cycle repeated itself once again.

If Marañón's portrait of the Count-Duke was shaped by the psychological theories of the period in which it was written, it was also influenced by the political circumstances of the time. The Europe of the 1920s and 1930s was the Europe of the dictators, and the rise of Mussolini and Hitler – again two contrasting physical types – surely provided him with a clue. Men with a 'passion to command' – and he conceded that there were many of them – could become dictators when they found themselves in a 'socially favourable environment'. 'It is then', he wrote, 'that the *caudillo*, the dictator, the leader of multitudes, appears.'[12] It is not, therefore, surprising to find the pyknic morphology of Olivares and the asthenic morphology of Richelieu discussed in his book under the subheading of 'the two archetypes of dictators'.[13] The rival seventeenth-century statesmen are transformed into twentieth-century-style dictators, whose inner drive for power converged with a 'socially favourable environment'.

Given the intellectual and political conditions that helped to shape it, Marañón's book was inevitably beginning to look dated when I first came across it in 1952. As a dissection of the Count-Duke's personality it was, and remains, a fascinating work, even if, as I immersed myself in the contemporary documentation, I was not necessarily persuaded by Marañón's retrospective diagnosis of his patient's ills. The mood swings were obvious, although it seemed to me that they might just as well be explained by the arrival of some piece of bad news from foreign parts, or a devastating personal event like the death of his only child, as by the mysteries of morphology. I also came to be as impressed by Olivares's determination to keep his emotions under control – a determination forged out of a combination of Christian resignation and neo-Stoic fortitude – as by the strength of the emotions themselves. I was equally unconvinced by Marañón's attempt to equate seventeenth-century statesmen, with their very limited means of arousing and leading the masses, with twentieth-century European dictators, who were in a position to benefit from all the resources of modern technology.

Above all, although Marañón cast a flood of light on the Count-Duke's personal relations with his monarch, his fellow nobles and members of his own immediate circle, the ways in which a 'socially favourable environment' enabled him to capture power and then hold on to it were far from clear, while the political environment received only the sketchiest attention. This was where I felt that it was still possible to make a useful contribution. The existence of Marañón's book absolved me from the need to adopt a conventional biographical approach and explore in depth my subject's personality. This had already been done and, even if I was not always persuaded by Marañón's interpretation, I doubted whether it would be possible to dig any deeper or produce a more convincing personal portrait.

The awareness of this left me free to concentrate on what most interested me – the problems of a great power at a moment of perceived decline. But was a biographical approach the best way of getting at the underlying question? As far as the historians of the *Annales* school were concerned, the answer was clearly in the negative. But I was troubled by

Braudel's depiction of Philip II as no more than the prisoner of great impersonal forces, and felt that the contemporary fashion for concentrating on long-term economic and social trends was in danger of turning the past into a series of abstractions. While recognizing the constraints imposed on statesmen by the social and economic environment in which they operated, I thought it dangerous to underestimate the power of human agency. Indeed, for me much of the fascination of the past lies in observing the continuous interplay between the individual and his or her environment. This environment, moreover, should not be limited to 'society' and the economy, but should include culture, and what came to be known as *mentalités*, a topic to which the *Annales* school would pay increasing attention in its post-Braudelian phase. I could see no good reason why social and economic circumstances should be regarded as somehow more 'fundamental' than human attitudes, behaviour and cultural conditioning.[14]

No doubt my own cultural conditioning, including perhaps the influence of Herbert Butterfield on my thinking at a formative stage in my development as a historian, made me sceptical of Marxist and *marxisant* interpretations of the past, even while attracted by their broad sweep and explanatory power. I never had any doubt that space should be found in any study of the past for human agency, personality, and what Harold Macmillan famously called 'events, dear boy, events'. Contingency – an unexpected death, the arrival or non-arrival of an important letter – should never be left out of account in the reconstruction and explanation of the past. On the other hand, historical study requires something more than the mere chronicling of events – 'surface disturbances' as Braudel disparagingly described them.[15] The challenge that confronts any ambitious historian is to capture the characteristics of an age in ways that make human actions and behaviour comprehensible, blending analysis and description without disrupting the narrative flow. In the end, as all good historians know, there will always be a sense of disappointment. No narrative is ever fully comprehensive, no explanation total, and the balance between description and analysis is painfully elusive. The best that can be hoped for is as close an approximation to a plausible reconstruction of past periods, people and events as the surviving evidence allows – a reconstruction, moreover, that is so effectively presented as to draw the reader in and on.

As far as I was concerned, the case for approaching the problems of seventeenth-century Spain through the biography of a principal actor was reinforced by the current state of the historiography of the period. Although much of this was, by modern standards, inadequate, I was fortunate in that certain aspects of it were currently receiving close attention from two or three outstanding contemporary Spanish historians who were just coming into their own. In 1960 Antonio Domínguez Ortiz, with whom I had enjoyed so many conversations in Simancas, published the study of Philip IV's finances that Braudel had wanted me to write.[16] While Domínguez Ortiz's conclusions would in due course be supplemented and refined, not least by the economic historian Felipe Ruiz Martín, who had worked in Paris with Braudel and would spend a year with me in Princeton, his book offered a panoramic survey of the state of the crown's finances and the fiscal policies of the Olivares regime which provided an essential starting-point for my own work. Domínguez Ortiz also published between 1963 and 1970 two impressively researched volumes on seventeenth-century Spanish society, dealing respectively with the aristocracy and the clergy.[17] Meanwhile, Spain's leading historian of ideas in the second half of the twentieth century, José Antonio Maravall, was publishing the results of his intensive reading in the literature of the Golden Age in a succession of articles and books that would culminate in a highly influential, if controversial, study of culture in the age of the baroque.[18]

These various publications meant that, whatever focus I eventually decided to choose for my own book, there was much more background material available for me than there had been when I began research in the 1950s on the Count-Duke and his Catalan policies. On the other hand, enormous gaps remained in our knowledge. Not only was relatively little information available about even some of the major political figures of the period, but the course of events itself was often far from clear, and without a basic chronology it is impossible to begin to discover how and why things happen as they do. While I had no enthusiasm for diplomatic history, about which Herbert Butterfield held ambivalent views, my realization of the importance of establishing the exact sequence of events enabled me to appreciate his insistence that there was no better training for a young historian than the analysis of a set of intricate diplomatic negotiations.[19] By concentrating on the development of the Count-Duke's policies towards France or England, and monitoring the flow of despatches into and out of Madrid, I would at least get a clearer sense of day-to-day developments that could lead to peace or war. Beyond this, I needed to know why important decisions were taken or not taken, and, in so far as policy was in the hands of the Count-Duke, it was likely to be in his papers, letters and speeches that many of the essential clues were to be found.

The various considerations prompted by the current state of the historiography of the Spain of Philip IV strengthened my conviction that at that particular moment the best way of approaching the problems of the period was through a study of the ministerial career of the dominant political figure of the reign, the Count-Duke. At the same time I was uneasily aware of the dangers of the 'great man' approach to the study of the past. As the principal focus of the biographer's attention he bestrides the stage. But was he as commanding a figure in life as he appears in retrospect? Is the contribution made by his colleagues, advisers and adjutants being underplayed? Can he be seen as representing the values and beliefs of his generation, or at least of its elite or a section of it, or do his attitudes and actions diverge in significant ways from the norm? There is no easy answer to such questions, and they are bound to raise doubts about the validity of a biographical approach.

There is, too, the matter of impartiality. In order to understand the motivations and behaviour of a Napoleon or a Philip II it is essential to enter as closely as possible into their

mind-sets. These will be conditioned by a whole range of influences – family background and social environment, upbringing
and education, personality and temperament, and all the experiences of daily life. The only way for biographers to get close to
a mind-set is to live mentally in the company of their subjects,
soaking themselves in their letters and papers and all the scraps
of information that cast light on their lives. But to live so inti-
mately with figures from the past is inevitably to some extent to
see the world through their eyes. While empathy is an essential
part of the art of biography, empathy can all too easily slide into
unwary sympathy. For me, as for so many of his contemporaries,
the Count-Duke was an overbearing and antipathetic character,
but as I tried to go through in my own mind the options facing
him – for instance, over whether or not to make a peace settlement with the Dutch – I found myself sharing his dilemmas
and trying to solve his problems for him. At this point the biographer is in danger of being trapped into a possibly unwarranted
degree of sympathy. To get inside the subject's skin and yet
maintain objectivity remains a constant challenge.

Where political biography is concerned, the temptation is
not only to see the world through the subject's own eyes, but
also to mould the narrative to conform to the patterns of his
life. There are many ways in which a historian can shape the
account of a period or a reign. My prime concern in a book
that was built around the Count-Duke's policies was to illustrate the eventual incompatibility between his determination
to restore Spain's international standing and his ambitious
programme for domestic reform. From this perspective the

turning-point of the reign seemed to me to come in 1628, when he decided in favour of military intervention in the dispute over the Mantuan succession – a decision that led inexorably to the sacrifice of his reform programme to the demands of war. An economic or social historian, on the other hand, might choose to locate the turning-point in approximately the same period, but attribute it to the agricultural and commercial depression of the years around 1630.

A political biography, by its nature, tends to neglect or exclude those elements and events that for one reason or another fall beyond the purview of the principal actor, and the actual writing of the book made me increasingly aware of how much I was having to leave out. Fortunately, however, opportunities arose that allowed me to cover elsewhere aspects of the period which I was unable to discuss at length within the confines of a single volume. Cambridge University invited me to be its Trevelyan Lecturer for 1982–3, and I chose as my subject a comparative study of Richelieu and Olivares as rival statesmen. This allowed me not only to explore the relationship of the two men in some detail, but also, and more importantly, to examine the differences between them and what they had in common. A closer acquaintance with Richelieu and the France of Louis XIII gave me a wider perspective on Olivares and his problems, lifting him out of an exclusively Spanish context and offering insights into the ways in which his problems and responses were conditioned by the times, and by the shared European civilization of which Spain formed a part.[20]

I also became aware, in talking to the many art historians in Princeton, and in particular to the leading Velázquez expert in the United States, Jonathan Brown, of the enormous importance of visual images as expressions of political intentions and ideas. It became clear to me that these images had to be set into the rich context of Spanish court culture, which I lacked the space to explore in any depth. The visual imagery and the context in which it was produced seemed to me to be of such historical importance as to deserve treatment on their own. The outcome was a collaborative book on the pleasure palace of the Buen Retiro, built by Olivares for his monarch on the outskirts of Madrid.[21]

I came to see, as I continued intermittent work on the biography while taking time off to explore these other aspects of the period, that the biography itself should be conceived of as part of a larger enterprise. The editing of some of Olivares's most important state papers, the comparison of his policies with those of his French rival, and a monograph on the cultural programme that he promoted at the court of Philip IV – all these, when taken together, made possible a more wide-ranging view of two decades of Spanish and European history than could be provided by a biography alone. To some extent this countered, at least in my own mind, some of the criticisms that can reasonably be levelled at a purely biographical approach to the history of an age. On the other hand, it could equally well be argued that the effect was to weaken the biography – for example, by reducing the amount of space that it should ideally have devoted to the Count-Duke's patronage of culture.[22]

What from one perspective, therefore, may look like an enrichment, can from another appear as a detraction. If I regarded my own approach as being the former, this was because, in the final analysis, I was less interested in the man than in a society, a culture and an age, and saw the biography as a means to an end rather than as an end in itself. Biographies are all too often called 'definitive', but the label is misleading, whether applied to a biography or to any other form of history. All historical enterprises are in fact work in progress – work that constitutes a form of collaboration across the generations. Over the course of time not only do more facts tend to be uncovered, but the preoccupations of a new generation can open up quite new perspectives on topics about which it was once thought that the last word had been said.

For my own part I saw my study of the Count-Duke's political career not as a form of closure but as a starting-point for others, and I hoped that my findings, while answering some questions, would help to raise others – in particular, questions capable of suggesting new lines of inquiry. It became obvious, for instance, during the course of my researches that Olivares himself needed to be seen in the context of an increasingly powerful family network centred on the interrelated houses of Guzmán, Zúñiga and Haro. The family connection proved strong enough to survive the fall from power of its most prominent member in 1643, and indeed managed to remain at the centre of government for another generation. The political history of the entire reign of Philip IV, from 1621 to 1665, could thus be written in terms of the dominance of a group of families, rather than of two related individuals, Olivares and his nephew Don Luis de Haro, his successor in the royal favour. Such an approach would seek to show how the various members of the network took advantage of the opportunities afforded them by their privileged access to the centre of power. Political dominance created or consolidated social and economic dominance, and could transform a family's fortunes.

Since the extended family stood at the centre of early modern European life, any divorce of political from social and economic history is artificial. An enhanced awareness of this over the past few decades has made old-style political history, with its emphasis on the role of one or two leading actors and on high politics conducted in a vacuum, appear increasingly anachronistic. Yet in any account of an age that aims to achieve some sort of completeness, politics and decision-making cannot be disregarded, even if they should not be seen as autonomous processes. But how can high politics be successfully related to the social, economic and cultural context in which it was conducted? If the biography of a single individual has obvious weaknesses as a device for achieving this kind of integration, collective biography, or prosopography, has sometimes seemed a more promising alternative.

A prosopographical approach requires the reconstruction not of one life but of many, or at least of those selected aspects of a cluster of lives that lend themselves to comparative analysis. This type of analysis, which is designed to explore the common characteristics and activities of a particular cohort or group and identify such connections as may have existed between its members, became highly influential in the 1920s and 1930s, and in the world of Anglo-American historical scholarship is associated in particular with the names of Lewis Namier (1888–1960) and Ronald Syme (1903–89). Syme's classic revision of the life and reign of the Emperor Augustus, *The Roman Revolution*, was published in 1939, and built on the work done by German historians of the late nineteenth and early twentieth centuries who had collected and assembled such pieces of biographical information as could be found about the principal players in the Roman political arena. In his introduction to the book Syme spelled out the case for a collective, prosopographical, approach. 'Undue insistence', he wrote, 'upon the character and exploits of a single person invests history with dramatic unity at the expense of truth. However talented and powerful in himself, the Roman statesman cannot stand alone, without allies, without a following ... The career of the revolutionary leader is fantastic and unreal if told without some indication of the composition of the faction he led, of the personality, actions and influence of the principal among his partisans. In all ages, whatever the form and name of government ... an oligarchy lurks behind the facade; and Roman history, Republican or Imperial, is the history of the governing class.'[23]

This same insight informed the reconstruction of eighteenth-century British political and parliamentary history by Lewis Namier and his colleagues and assistants.[24] It is hardly a coincidence that the analysis of ruling elites came into fashion at a time when both the present and the past were being interpreted in terms of class conflict and class interest. The oligarchy that dominated British political and social life in the eighteenth century provided a perfect case study for this kind of approach, and Namier's work was to prove highly influential in the decades following the Second World War. Requiring as it did the painstaking reconstruction of a multitude of individual lives through the unearthing and piecing together of an infinity of details about the family background, life and activities of members of the House of Commons, Namier's methodology, although bearing the stamp of his own genius, derived in direct line of descent from the *Dictionary of National Biography*, with its more than 29,000 entries. Indeed, the editor of that great enterprise himself foresaw in 1896 the potential contribution of the *Dictionary* to what would one day come to be called the 'namierization' of eighteenth-century party politics.[25] As is customary in historical writing, each generation stands on the shoulders of its predecessors, and each new accomplishment provides an occasion for new insights.

Namierization, however, although making an immense contribution to the sociological understanding of the eighteenth-century British elite or at least an important section of it, was to have its limitations as a blanket device for understanding the motivations of politicians and the decision-making process. As Namier himself was acutely aware, kinship and clientage are no infallible guarantee of political loyalty. If, for instance, a study of the three dominant families in the Spain of Philip IV were to be undertaken, it would show how personal rivalries, family feuds and the sheer instinct for survival all helped to fracture and undermine the solidarity of what on the surface appeared to be an all-powerful family connection. On the other hand, the study of these feuds and fissures cannot necessarily of itself provide the key that will unlock the politics of an age. Namier's preoccupation with uncovering the intricacies of such family and personal relationships led to accusations that he had left the ideas out of politics and reduced everything to 'interest'. But ideology as a driving force in political life is never in fact a constant, and the relative importance of 'interest' and ideas is liable to vary from one period to another. In periods where no great issues appear to divide the political nation, factions and family alignments may assume greater importance than at other times, and an extreme degree of political management may be needed to supply some of the coherence that can otherwise be at least partly provided by political conviction.

Such conviction emerges from a set of ideas and values that require just as much study as the alignments of family and faction whose importance was central to the political life of early modern societies. The attempt to identify and analyse these ideas and values has been given a fresh impetus by the 'linguistic turn' of recent years, which has made historians increasingly sensitive to the use of the language of earlier generations, and also to that of their own.[26] As I studied Golden Age Spain it was borne in on me how frequently the word 'reputación' surfaced in the political literature of the period and in the discussions of the Spanish Council of State. 'Reputación', as used by the councillors, was bound up with the complex notions of honour that prevailed in early modern societies, and involved the standing and reputation of Spain and its monarch in the eyes both of contemporaries and of posterity. The councillors were acutely aware of the importance of reputation – of not losing face – and the concept was central to the shaping of foreign-policy decisions in sixteenth- and seventeenth-century Spain.[27]

The isolation and examination of key words, such as 'reputation', 'conservation' and 'reformation' in the Spain of the seventeenth century, can provide important clues to the attitudes and thought processes of a statesman or of a political elite.[28] But the power inherent in those words and in the concepts behind them are closely related to their wider resonance and possibly contested uses in society at large, which in turn call for examination. In so far as they have a resonance they also lend themselves to manipulation by astute politicians. The deployment of the word 'reputation' by Olivares was a useful device for discrediting the regime of his predecessor, the Duke of Lerma, whose policies could be depicted as destroying the *reputación* of his monarch and the Spanish Monarchy – a charge that could be counted upon to touch a sensitive chord in an acutely honour-conscious society.

However politically motivated the deployment of a distinctive vocabulary, it draws its strength from the conceptual world from which it emerges, and an awareness of the nature of that conceptual world is essential for any reconstruction of the intentions of a political leader or leaders. Their world-view, and that of their generation, will be shaped not only by family background and personal experience, but also by the form and content of their education, their religion (or the absence of it) and their reading. As the history of books and of reading has become an increasingly popular subject of study among historians, library catalogues have been subjected to close critical scrutiny.[29] But it is generally recognized that the clues given by the contents of a library to the mental world of its owner need to be treated with great caution. How many of the books on its shelves were inherited or came as gifts, and how many of them had the owner actually read? The Count-Duke was a passionate bibliophile and assembled one of the great personal libraries of the seventeenth century, but, although he enjoyed discussions with learned men, we have no indication of how many of the books in his library, and which particular ones, he found time to read.[30]

It is, however, possible through the examination of booksellers' inventories and the study of printing and the book trade to get some idea of the relative popularity of different kinds of books and gauge their impact on society. There are many indications, for instance, that post-Tridentine Catholicism and the neo-Stoic writings of Justus Lipsius exercised an important influence over the generation of educated Frenchmen and Spaniards to which Richelieu and Olivares belonged.[31] It is not, therefore, surprising to find them harping in their papers and correspondence on such Lipsian concepts as discipline, authority and order. These concepts, widely diffused among their contemporaries, not only helped to shape their mental world but could also be used to endow their actions with legitimacy.

Yet the context in which political action occurs is not defined exclusively by concepts and the vocabulary through which they find expression. It is also shaped by a political and social environment that, like words and concepts, changes over time. In the monarchical societies of early modern Europe it was the monarch who stood at the apex of power. It was while working on seventeenth-century Catalonia that the constant repetition in contemporary petitions of two words, 'servicio' and 'merced' – service and favour – forcefully brought home to me the way in which early modern European societies were structured around the reciprocal nature of social relationships, and how these found their ultimate resolution in the person of the monarch.[32] It was incumbent on vassals to render loyal service to their monarch, but it was no less incumbent on the monarch to reward the services of loyal vassals with tangible signs of favour. They in turn were expected to pass on some share of the benefits accruing from royal favour to their own relatives and dependants, likewise as a reward for services rendered or anticipated. The process would be repeated down the social scale, diminishing as it went. Patronage in these societies conferred power, and the ultimate source of patronage and power was the person of the monarch. It was through the judicious exercise of patronage, backed up by royal authority and in the last resort by military force, that the successful monarch ensured obedience to his or her commands and fulfilled the tasks of government.

Kingship was therefore central to the working of the political system in these monarchical, hierarchically organized societies, whose political and social ordering was seen as replicating a cosmic order regulated and ordained by an omnipotent Creator. The extravagant language in which a Richelieu or an Olivares addressed his monarch, the servility and sheer abasement of those who served a ruler or gained entry to the royal presence, vividly reflected prevailing views about the divine character and origins of royal authority – views that would come to be challenged and contested, but that would for long continue to permeate the monarchical societies of early modern Europe.

It is not easy for the largely undeferential western societies of today to recapture the traditional aura of monarchy, and it requires a leap of the imagination to enter a vanished world. Not surprisingly, as that world recedes further and further into the past, so the phenomenon of kingship has come increasingly to attract the attention of historians, although, in this, as in so much else, they have tended to lag behind their anthropological colleagues. What was once taken for granted now has to be both explored and explained. Although the modern study of kingship by historians possesses a long prehistory, it was effectively shaped in the second half of the twentieth century by Ernst Kantorowicz's enormously influential study *The King's Two Bodies*, first published in 1957.[33] In tracing the origins and development in medieval Christendom of the fiction of the simultaneously divine and human nature of kingship, Kantorowicz indicated new ways of exploring the character, operation and manifestations of monarchical power. The fact that the human and the divine were perceived as uniting in the person of the monarch made it clear that any study of the actions of a ruler could no longer properly be divorced from the ritual and pageantry that accompanied his or her person. Confirmation of the value and importance of such an approach was provided by the work of symbolic anthropologists, notably that of Clifford Geertz, whose depiction of the nineteenth-century Balinese 'theatre-state' showed how the deployment of symbols could be seen as integral to the functioning of society and the exercise of power.[34]

It could indeed be argued that, in the Geertzian view of society, symbols count for more than politics. But, as studies of court life and ceremonial have multiplied, political history has been forced to take increased account of the place occupied by ritual, symbolism and imagery in the political processes of early modern Europe, and of the way in which rulers and their advisers used and manipulated images in the attempt to enhance their power.[35] Even if the study of kingship has at times been in danger of being swamped by accounts of its representation, it has become clear that a knowledge of the court environment is indispensable for an understanding of the realities of early modern political activity.

An anthropological dissection of court rituals and royal pageantry, however, can all too easily result in a static picture of the past, and conceal the changes going on beneath the surface of even the most etiquette-bound of courts. New monarchs were liable to have their own agendas, and bring new men to power. Kingship itself evolved over the course of time, altering in response to changing circumstances, of which the most important in the early modern period was the Protestant Reformation, with the consequent division of the continent into rival religious groupings, and the rise of a major domestic challenge to the authority of monarchs created by the emergence of religious dissidents among their own subjects. In the sixteenth century religion became a double-edged weapon, offering a potentially lethal threat to monarchical authority when placed in the hands of dissidents, but simultaneously allowing monarchs themselves to enhance and reinforce their authority by insisting on the indissoluble union of throne and altar and their own divinely ordained mission. [36]

Other important changes, however, were also under way, and the fact that I should have devoted a large amount of time and energy to a political biography not of Philip IV of Spain but of one of his subjects is symptomatic of the shifting political scene. While the monarch was, and remained, at the apex of power, the processes of government were becoming more time-consuming, and the management of patronage more complex. Royal councillors had always been a fact of political life, and monarchs had always had their favourites, but the early seventeenth century saw the emergence of a number of powerful figures in the courts of Europe who combined in their persons the characteristics of councillors and favourites, and helped to relieve their royal masters of some of the burdens that kings were called upon to bear. Neither exactly old-style favourites nor modern-style prime ministers, these figures – Richelieu in France, the Duke of Lerma and the Count-Duke of Olivares in Spain, the Duke of Buckingham in England – have come to be known as 'minister-favourites'.

In 1963, well before I settled down to write about Olivares, the distinguished Spanish legal historian Francisco Tomás Valiente, whose life was cruelly cut short by terrorists in 1996, published a ground-breaking institutional study of the favourite – the *privado* or *valido* – as the central figure in the government of seventeenth-century Spain.[37] Eleven years later a French historian of central Europe, Jean Bérenger, suggested that historians of the seventeenth century should see, and study, minister-favourites not just in a national context but as a 'European phenomenon'.[38] Bérenger had thrown down a challenge, and a colleague and I decided to take it up by organizing a conference in Oxford designed to do exactly this. The resulting book, published in 1999, although far from being comprehensive, underlined the extent of the phenomenon, and also suggested some of the possibilities, as well as the difficulties, of examining it on a comparative basis.[39] Conditions varied widely from country to country and court to court, and it is far from clear whether the emergence of a minister-favourite, or a figure approximating him, was the effect of a similar set of circumstances, or the consequence of a particular local situation. Nor is it entirely clear why the era of the minister-favourite should have been relatively transitory, with monarchs seeking after 1660 to reassert their personal authority, although not always with success.

Yet the conference, and the book to which it gave rise, helped draw attention to the political, social and cultural importance of figures who had tended to be dismissed by nineteenth-century historians as owing their prominence to no more than the personal weaknesses or foibles of the monarchs, like James I of England or Philip III of Spain, who raised them up to greatness. The fact that a cluster of them emerged around the turn of the sixteenth and seventeenth centuries, and that they became the objects of such universal obloquy, raises a set of historical problems that are far from being solved. Their solution, when it comes, will not come from old-style political history, conceived in narrow institutional terms. Nor will it come from a purely biographical approach that tends to look to personality as providing the essential answers.

Political history and biography still have much to offer, but the way in which the study of the past has developed over the course of the last half-century has potentially created a richness of context that I could scarcely have envisaged when I set out to write *The Count-Duke of Olivares*.[40] The publication of that book in 1986 may have contributed to a greater acceptance, especially in Spain itself, of the value of a biographical approach to the understanding of the past, and it is a sign of changing attitudes that the absence of a Spanish dictionary of national biography, which I have so long lamented both in private and in public, has finally been remedied by the publication by Spain's Royal Academy of History of a fifty-volume work modelled on the *Oxford Dictionary of National Biography*.[41]

The possibilities of an enriched political history are great, but so too are the technical difficulties, and each historian will need to find his or her own way through the maze. Imagination, empathy, the ability to master a wide range of diverse kinds of evidence – all these will need to be brought into play if political actors are to be convincingly related to the social, conceptual and political world which shaped them and which they in turn sought to shape.

CHAPTER FOUR

Perceptions of decline

IN 1962 the British journalist and author Anthony Sampson published *Anatomy of Britain*, a critical and highly influential study of the institutions by which post-war Britain was being governed, and of the people who ran them. The book's success led to a substantially revised edition nine years later, entitled *The New Anatomy of Britain*. During those years there had been an intensifying debate about the status of post-war and post-imperial Britain – in particular about its relations with Europe and the United States, and its capacity to meet the challenges of a changing world. On opening this revised version of the *Anatomy* I was startled to see that the three citations used as epigraphs to the first edition – taken from Walter Bagehot, Amiel and the Duke of Edinburgh respectively – had been replaced by a sentence of my own. The sentence in question pronounced my verdict on the attitudes and assumptions of the seventeenth-century Spanish elite: 'Heirs to a society which had over-invested in empire, and surrounded by the increasingly shabby remnants of a dwindling inheritance, they could not bring themselves at the moment of crisis to surrender their memories and alter the antique pattern of their lives.'[1]

Much of the public debate in Britain between the 1960s and the 1980s revolved, openly or tacitly, around the theme of decline – whether the country which had emerged victorious from the Second World War and had seemed for a time to be recovering well from the strains of the conflict might now be slipping into decline. If it was, what were the causes, and how, if it could not be reversed, could the process of decline at least be managed?[2] The sentence in *Imperial Spain*, published a year after the first edition of *Anatomy of Britain*, had clearly struck a chord with the author, who found disturbing similarities between the outlook of the contemporary British elite and the elite of imperial Spain as it moved inexorably down the slope from national greatness and imperial power to second-rate status. Others, including leading politicians, would take up the Spanish analogy in the years that followed, and my words were still being resurrected in the 1980s.[3]

The publicity given in post-war Britain to a sentence in a book describing the experiences of a very different society three centuries earlier vividly illustrates the way in which the past and the present constantly, and sometimes unexpectedly, interact. Similarities, real or imaginary, are noticed, parallels are drawn, and the past becomes an arsenal that supplies weapons for contemporary debate. But the process moves in both directions, since contemporary preoccupations are liable to inform the choices of historians as they identify topics for research.

Sometimes the process is open and explicit. It is no accident that Paul Kennedy, whose *The Rise and Fall of the Great Powers* became a publishing sensation when it first appeared in 1987, should have asked me to contribute an essay about Olivares, entitled 'Managing Decline', to a volume of essays devoted to 'grand strategies'.[4] His request came at the moment when Mrs Thatcher was attempting to reverse the process of perceived decline in Great Britain, and when Americans, for their part, were beginning to worry that the United States might now be set on the downward path already trodden by Britain, Spain and ancient Rome. Indeed, much of the success of Kennedy's *Rise and Fall* among American readers may be attributed to the belief that a knowledge of the history of past empires might enable them to predict what the future held in store for their own society.

If, as in these instances, there is an explicit correlation between the work of historians and the contemporary preoccupations of their own societies, at other times the correlation may be partially or totally hidden, even from themselves. *Imperial Spain* was the work of a young historian living in post-imperial Britain. I had been brought up in a world in which large parts of the map were still painted red, and in which, even if the Second World War had seen the definitive replacement of British global hegemony by that of the United States, the superiority of British culture, values and ideals was still largely taken for granted by the generation that preceded my own. If at that time, as the political columnist Peter Jenkins noted in *Mrs. Thatcher's Revolution*, 'the word "decline" was uncongenial to the governing class, the thought of it had not escaped its mind'. For him, the words I used to describe the state of mind of the seventeenth-century Spanish elite were 'clearly intended to have contemporary relevance'.[5] I am not sure that this is correct, but I was writing in the wake of the Suez crisis, and my feelings about the mind-set of those who took Britain into its last imperial venture may well have coloured my views. In any event, the awareness that I belonged to the first post-imperial generation of my countrymen must have played some part in directing my attention, and at times my sympathies, to the struggles of a generation of Spaniards who, centuries earlier, had been confronted with a set of circumstances that were not entirely dissimilar to our own.

Yet my chosen field of research can hardly be described as a new one, even if, as I came to feel, it had been inadequately handled. 'The decline of Spain' was a standard topic in historical literature, and historians had long been attempting to identify its causes. At the time I began my research, far and away the most influential of recent attempts was an article published in 1938 by the American economic historian Earl J. Hamilton, who, in the age of Keynes, had made his name with an impressively documented study of the inflationary consequences of the arrival in Spain of vast quantities of silver from the mines of Mexico and Peru.[6] Since then, some of Hamilton's assumptions and conclusions about the impact of American bullion on the economy of Spain and Europe had been questioned, while new publications had appeared on aspects of Spanish economic and social life which suggested the need for a revision and amplification of his arguments. I set out to provide these in an essay published in *Past and Present* in 1961, which deliberately carried the same title, 'The Decline of Spain', as Hamilton's article.[7]

The problem of decline, which Hamilton treated as primarily an economic phenomenon, needs to be set in a larger historiographical context. At its most expansive it embraces entire civilizations, with cultural decline as an important element in the story. It also embraces the rise and fall of states and empires, which may, as with the Roman Empire, come to be treated as coterminous with civilization itself. As one of the oldest and most traditional of master-narratives, the conceptualization of the past in terms of the rise and fall of empires has retained its centrality from biblical times to our own. Even if its nature remains ill-defined and nebulous,[8] power has always engaged the interest of historians, who rarely possess it, and the rise and fall of states is the story of the acquisition and loss of power, which may be conceived of as military, political, economic or cultural, or, more frequently, as a combination of all four. In writing his *Decline and Fall of the Roman Empire*, Edward Gibbon stood in a long line of writers, thinkers and prophets within the Judeo-Christian and classical traditions. This stretched back through the Renaissance historians and medieval chroniclers like Otto of Freising to St Augustine, and before him to the great Roman historians and Polybius, with his cycles of rise and decline, and still further back to the prophet Daniel and his succession of four empires.[9]

The history of Spain between the late fifteenth and the late seventeenth centuries stands squarely within this master-narrative of the rise and decline of empires, which indeed itself came to influence contemporary perceptions of Spanish imperial power. For Spain, as for Rome before it and for Britain later, the history of both rise and decline raises fundamental questions about the character of states and societies, the impact on them of geography and environment, the relationship of economic strength to military might and cultural creativity, the nature of the goals a society sets itself, and the internal and external circumstances that determine its degree of success in attaining those goals.

The Harvard historian Roger B. Merriman, who published between 1918 and 1934 his grand narrative *The Rise of the Spanish Empire in the Old World and the New*,[10] permitted himself, at the end of his four volumes, a few reflections on the causes of the decline of the empire whose rise he had so carefully chronicled. In his view it was 'the very continuity of [Spain's] imperial tradition that furnishes the chief explanation of the suddenness of her rise and of her fall', but he had to confess that the fall was 'the product of a complex of different causes; and we are still quite as far from . . . having reached any general agreement as to the relative importance of those that have already been assigned, as we are in the case of those that have been given for the fall of Rome'.[11]

The search for the causes of decline – Roman, Spanish, British – can all too easily assume the characteristics of a historical parlour game, in which a variety of possible causes – economic, demographic, social, political – are paraded and then ranked in order, in accordance with the proclivities of the author and the temper of the times. One difficulty with this approach is that the very concept of decline – the Latin 'declinatio' or 'inclinatio' – is shrouded in confusion and uncertainty. Decline implies a falling away, but *from* what and *of* what? It is a concept that can be fitted neatly into a cyclical view of time – a view that finds endorsement in the processes of the natural world and the human body, with its successive stages of birth, growth, maturity and decay. It was not difficult to draw an analogy between the life cycle of the human body and that of the body politic. Yet a linear view of time may operate to the same effect as a cyclical one. Although it may point towards progress and development, it can equally well point in the opposite direction: Hesiod's golden age turns into an age of silver, and thence to baser metals. In the multiple and often conflicting sources embedded within the western tradition there were ample opportunities for an interpretation of the past couched in terms of rise followed by inexorable decline, although Christianity, by allowing for the possibility of divine intervention, was always at hand to challenge the excesses of determinism.[12]

Rise and decline is therefore one of the stories that societies and civilizations tell about themselves. It is a story that is not confined to the western world, as *The Muqaddimah* of the great fourteenth-century Arab historian Ibn Khaldûn so brilliantly reveals.[13] It has, however, permeated western thinking about the past and present, although with greater intensity in some periods than in others. Renaissance and post-Renaissance Europe looked back on the period since the end of the Roman Empire, or alternatively of the Roman Republic, as an age of decline, but it also glimpsed the possibilities of a new upwards movement as it came to realize that in some fields of activity the moderns were showing themselves the superiors of the ancients. In the eighteenth century the notion of decline, whether cyclical or permanent, was powerfully challenged by a fully minted idea of progress.[14] This in turn, however, was in due course to provoke a reaction. Even at the height of the age of industrialization and the global dominance of the west, triumphalist assertions of the inevitable progress of science, technology and reason called forth a response in the countervailing idea of decadence, which at least in some later nineteenth-century circles had its own appeal.[15] Nor did the idea of progress ever fully recover from the catastrophe of the First World War.

Cataclysmic times give birth to prophets of doom, and provide a ready audience for their predictions and beliefs. Oswald Spengler, with his *Decline of the West*, of 1918–22, spoke to the deep-seated anxieties of a western world shaken by the carnage of the recent conflict and haunted by forebodings as to what the future promised.[16] In equating the life cycle of civilizations with that of living organisms doomed to decay and extinction, Spengler, although speaking from the standpoint of the 1920s, was harping on an ancient theme. Yet even as he was brooding on the inevitability of the downfall of the west, the great Dutch historian Johan Huizinga, in *The Waning of the Middle Ages* (1924), one of the most influential works of twentieth-century history, was telling a story of decline that also ended as a story of renewal: 'a high and strong culture is declining, but at the same time and in the same sphere new things are being born'.[17]

For all its final note of hope, the notion of decline dominated Huizinga's account, as it also dominated Arnold Toynbee's enormously ambitious twelve-volume *A Study of History* (1934–61), with its bold attempt to systematize the trajectories of a wide range of somewhat ill-defined 'civilizations'. Even if he rejected Spenglerian notions of cyclical rise and decline in favour of his own theory of challenge and response, which in principle would allow civilizations and societies to transcend their moments of crisis and thus prolong their existence, Toynbee's message was at best uncertain about the west's future prospects. More important in terms of the reception of his work than any sliver of hope it may have proffered was the fact that it appeared to establish a set of laws that, once understood, could be seen as governing the whole of human history. The result was a predictability about both the past and the future that gave the work, at least in a digested form, its popular appeal. It certainly bowled me over when I read the abridged version while on military service, the year before going up to university.[18] Yet I was left feeling uneasy about Toynbee's escape mechanism from the dead-end of determinism, as formulated in his famous thesis of 'challenge and response'. How challenging does a challenge have to be to

call forth an adequate response, and how is it that some societies respond successfully to the challenges that confront them
while others do not? It was difficult not to feel that Toynbee's
formula, instead of solving the problem of rise and decline, did
nothing more than carry it one stage further back.[19]

Although the formidable shadows of Spengler and Toynbee
loomed in the background of mid-twentieth-century discussions of the rise and fall of states, much of the running in the
period following the Second World War was made by economic
historians and by social and political scientists. Max Weber's
thesis about the relationship between Protestantism and capitalism was deployed to explain why some early modern states,
like the Dutch Republic, prospered while others, like Catholic
Spain, faltered and stagnated. The growing interest in the
history of entrepreneurship drew attention to the way in which
clusters of dynamic and strongly motivated individuals could
transform traditional societies, or at least those societies in
which conditions were sufficiently favourable to support their
sense of enterprise. Those societies, on the other hand, where
entrepreneurial values were unable to prevail found themselves
condemned to stagnation or decline.

This theme also attracted the attention of psychologists like
David C. McClelland, whose *The Achieving Society* looked at
the psychological factors requisite for economic development,
and attempted to evaluate theories about the rise and fall of
civilizations by using the methods of the behavioural sciences.[20]
This economic and social science literature, which certainly
influenced my own thinking at this time, played into some of

the contributions to Carlo Cipolla's *The Economic Decline of Empires*, an anthology which included my own 1961 article on the decline of Spain in addition to an extract on the same theme from Vicens Vives's *Economic History of Spain*.[21]

Yet even if recent and contemporary literature on the general theme of rise and decline helped shape my *Imperial Spain* and the way I was thinking about the Spanish seventeenth century, I was primarily influenced – and to some extent held prisoner – by the traditions of Spanish and European historiography. Foreign observers had been announcing, and in some cases anticipating, the decline of Spain from the late sixteenth century onwards.[22] By the second half of the seventeenth century the fact that Spain was in a state of decline had become a European commonplace: 'the Monarchy of Spain is fallen to a great declination', observed the instructions given to the new British envoy to Madrid in 1663.[23] The use of the word 'declination' is a testimonial to the way in which the organic concept of birth, growth and decay, together with Renaissance readings of the history of ancient Rome, had permeated European consciousness and given observers a framework in which to set contemporary developments.

The scene was thus set for the search for the possible causes of Spain's decline, with the proffered explanations ranging from the activities of the Inquisition and the expulsion of the Moriscos between 1609 and 1614 to incompetent government and innate Spanish characteristics, of which the most prominent were thought to be fanaticism, superstition and sloth – all three anathema to the age of the Enlightenment. The verdict of the *philosophes* on Spain was famously summed up in the article on Spain by Nicolas Masson de Morvilliers in the volume of the *Encyclopédie* devoted to 'modern geography', published in 1783: 'What do we owe to Spain? What has it done for Europe in the last two centuries, in the last four, or ten?'[24] This image of Spain as a backward and decadent country was thus firmly implanted in the collective European consciousness, where it has lingered almost until today.

Although Masson's damning pronouncements provoked a furious response from eighteenth-century Spanish authors, they also played into deep-seated anxieties about the past and the present of their country. While some felt that Spain had fallen behind and could only catch up by learning from its more successful European rivals, others preferred to dwell on the achievements and glories of its past.[25] The debate continued over the course of the nineteenth century, as liberal historians depicted the two centuries of Habsburg rule as the age in which absolutism had destroyed Spain's traditional liberties and religious intolerance had stunted its intellectual and scientific development, while their conservative opponents argued that involvement in Europe had been the source of all its woes, and that it had been at its greatest when it had been truest to itself. The political upheavals of nineteenth-century Spain did nothing to encourage the growth of national confidence, but a powerful new impetus was given to discussions over the country's presumed *decadencia* by the disasters of 1898, the year in which Spain, defeated in war by the United States, lost the remnants of its overseas empire, Cuba, Puerto Rico and the

Philippines. The humiliation of that defeat triggered a new round of national soul-searching, in which intellectuals, writers and historians – the so-called 'generation of 1898' – endlessly debated what came to be known as 'the problem of Spain'.[26]

Spain was in fact far from unique in its late nineteenth-century bout of soul-searching. The Spanish writer and reformer Joaquín Costa (1846–1911) was made fully aware of the extent of his country's intellectual, economic and social backwardness when he visited the Paris International Exhibition of 1867;[27] but that same exhibition also brought home to concerned members of the British ruling class that their country, the pioneer of industrialization, was now being overtaken by the Germans. The result was an anxious debate about the deficiencies of British education and technology.[28] Anxieties about the decline in the country's spirit of enterprise and technological skills were joined at the turn of the century by growing concern over Britain's military and naval capacity, caused by the shock of the Boer War and the accelerating German programme of naval rearmament. Meanwhile France, reeling from defeat in the Franco-Prussion War of 1870, turned inwards on itself in anguished debate over the causes of and possible cures for national decline,[29] just as Spain would do thirty years later in the wake of its shattering defeat in the Spanish-American War.

Although the perception of decline gives rise to deep-seated pessimism, it is also likely to generate calls for regeneration and reform. This happened in Spain, as in France and Britain, but to less effect. The generation of 1898 was very diverse in composition and outlook, and the remedies it advanced for the alleged national disease carried little political weight. Even the best-known contributors to the debate, like Miguel de Unamuno (1864–1936), José Ortega y Gasset (1883–1955), and that great defender of traditional Spain Marcelino Menéndez Pelayo (1856–1912) had a small readership by European standards, and Spain before the advent of the Second Republic in 1931 failed to grapple with the social, political and economic problems that were holding it back. As a result, the debate remained largely confined to the realm of analysis, and the analysis was in general superficial and repetitive. In the new age of psychoanalysis, explanations of the 'problem of Spain' centred in particular on what was assumed to be an unchanging national psyche. Joaquín Costa had declared himself 'inclined to think that the cause of our inferiority and our decadence is ethnic'.[30] Somehow it seemed as if a national character shaped by ethnic origin and historical circumstance in the more or less distant past had made Spaniards psychologically incapable of adapting to the modern world.

The Civil War brought to power a reactionary regime which, drawing on the conservative and clerical tradition, sought to reverse the terms of the debate by suggesting that it was the rest of the world, and not Spain, that was out of step. But for all the regime's high-flown pronouncements of Spain's fidelity to eternal values, the sense of inferiority persisted, and with it a narrative of the nation's past over which hovered like a spectre the shadow of decline. In the 1950s the 'problem of Spain' was at the heart of the fierce debate between two historical giants in exile, Américo Castro and Claudio Sánchez Albornoz, over the origins of the Spanish national temperament and the structure of Spanish history. True heirs of the generation of 1898, both of them took Spanish exceptionalism for granted, and both put forward essentialist explanations centred on the national psyche. Their battle was fought over which period of the Spanish past it was that gave birth to that psyche.[31]

I was not alone in finding this essentialist approach unconvincing, and had a long and difficult meeting with Américo Castro in Madrid after his return from exile, in which he upbraided me for the failure of British historians to appreciate his work. But there were also many good historians in the Spain of those years who either ignored, or had moved beyond, the essentialism that pervaded the work of these two antagonists. As Vicens Vives wrote in the prologue to his *Approaches to the History of Spain*, 'I would even go so far as to affirm that both of their methods have been largely superseded, although in doing so I am well aware that I will bring down upon myself fulminous rays from each Olympus.'[32] Yet the master-narrative of decline lived on. This was the narrative, supported by good historiography as well as bad, into which I unwittingly bought when I embarked on my researches, and it was the narrative that shaped my early work. The subtitle of *The Revolt of the Catalans: A Study in the Decline of Spain, 1598–1640* suggested itself almost automatically. It seemed a natural choice.

After examining and reassessing in my 1961 article 'The Decline of Spain' the various causes of decline adduced by Earl J. Hamilton, I concluded, 'It seems improbable that any account of the *decline of Spain* can substantially alter the commonly accepted version of seventeenth-century Spanish history, for there are always the same cards, however we shuffle them.' As I came to know more about the period, however, and read more widely in the writings of seventeenth-century Spaniards who expressed their own views on the state of their country, I began to realize that the story was perhaps rather more complicated than I had previously assumed. Hamilton had ended his article by referring to the writers, commonly known as *arbitristas*, who had commented on the predicament of Spain, and especially that of Castile, the homeland of the majority of them. 'History', he wrote, 'records few instances of either such able diagnosis of fatal social ills by any group of moral philosophers or of such utter disregard by statesmen of sound advice.'[33] More recently, the French Marxist historian Pierre Vilar had also drawn attention to the acuteness of some of these writers in a brilliant article on the Spain of Don Quixote, whom he saw as an emblematic figure for the Spain of his time.[34]

A growing acquaintance with the work of these moralists, projectors and reformers made me appreciate, in a way I had not previously appreciated, the intellectual dimension to the question of Spain's decline. Historians might retrospectively hunt for specific causes of decline in the economy, or society, or international rivalries, but the way in which contemporaries saw their own situation was itself a part of the story, and therefore needed to be taken into account. While they, too, hunted for causes, they were making their diagnoses and putting forward their remedies from within a mental world in which the fact of decline, and the process of decline, were taken as axiomatic. Ever since the Fall of Man, corruption had been innate in the world; the cyclical process of growth and decay affected every living organism; and the experience of past societies offered ample confirmation of the process over the course of human history.

It was above all to the history of Rome and its empire that these seventeenth-century Spaniards turned as they contemplated the situation in which they found themselves. Roman history was especially relevant because, in conquering a New World and dominating the Old, Spaniards had grown accustomed to thinking of themselves as the heirs to Rome.[35] But it began to occur to them that they might also turn out to be its heirs in other, less fortunate ways. The setbacks and military reverses suffered by Spain in the last years of the sixteenth century and the growing strains imposed on the Castilian economy and Castilian society by almost continuous warfare naturally encouraged contemporary moralists and commentators to predict that Spain was going the way of Rome. Finding in the writings of Roman historians some uncomfortable precedents for what seemed to be happening in their own society, they were not slow to sound the alarm. Belonging as they did to a Counter-Reformation society infused with the sense of sinfulness and guilt, they were particularly attracted to those historians of the Roman world, like Sallust and Paulus Orosius, a fifth-century Christian priest from Visigothic Spain, who looked to internal causes for the explanation of Rome's decline. Luxury, idleness and corruption had sapped its energies and undermined

Rome from within. But this pessimistic reading also carried a message of hope which had its appeal for Counter-Reformation society. By returning to the values that had originally inspired it, a diseased society might still be able to recover its health.[36]

As I read the works of these seventeenth-century writers, alongside the discussions among Spanish ministers about the course of action they should adopt in dealing with specific challenges, I began to realize the extent to which the making of policy in the Spain of Philip III and Philip IV was conditioned not so much by decline, whatever that might involve, as by the *perception* of decline. This realization inspired an article I published in 1977 on the theme of self-perception and decline in Spain,[37] and also helped inform my later study of the Count-Duke, in which I sought to present him as a statesman who saw himself as attempting to halt and reverse the decline that he believed was overtaking the Spanish Monarchy. The theme of decline, and in particular of moral decline, was in no sense a monopoly of Spain in the seventeenth century, but the intensity of the problems that were weighing down upon it, and the contrast between its present troubles and the run of successes which had made it the dominant power in Europe in the preceding century, made seventeenth-century Spaniards especially sensitive to presumed indications of decline.

If 'decline' can be regarded as a cultural construct that runs from Roman times to our own, this does not, however, make it a phenomenon unchanging over time. On the contrary, different societies and different ages will assess and measure it by differing yardsticks and criteria. The Spain of Olivares was deeply exercised by the contrast between the present and the past, although there was disagreement as to exactly when the heights were reached and the descent began. Was it in the reign of Philip II, or that of Ferdinand and Isabella, or perhaps in a remoter and idealized medieval past, when Castile still possessed the simple virtues and values of a warrior society engaged in a heroic crusade against Islam?

The contrast between past and present, however, was only one among possible criteria for determining whether, and to what extent, decline was under way. The international rivalries arising from the competitive state system of early modern Europe meant that states and societies instinctively measured their power and effectiveness against that of their rivals and neighbours. As discussion about the state and its sources of power acquired growing sophistication over the course of the sixteenth and seventeenth centuries, narrow comparisons about relative military or naval strength were extended to include the economic foundations of that strength, as measured by size of population, the buoyancy of commerce, and agricultural and industrial productivity. Economic backwardness in relation to other contemporary societies thus became an important criterion for assessing the weaknesses of one's own.

The notion of backwardness was a theme capable of almost indefinite extension. It could be made to embrace culture and the arts, as monarchs sought to outshine their rivals by making their courts the most brilliant in Europe, and it became increasingly important in the realm of science and technology. Already in the 1620s and 1630s Olivares was worrying about the technological backwardness, or, as he put it, the 'barbarism', of Spain in relation to engineering techniques that had been developed to improve internal navigation in other parts of Europe.[38] The eighteenth-century emphasis on the progress of science, reason and civilization only served to increase the anxieties of those societies that felt that they had fallen behind, or were in danger of doing so. Other criteria, like the possession of overseas empire, were subsequently brought into play, although it was only in the twentieth century that success in sport came to be regarded as an indicator of a nation's general state of health.

Is 'decline' therefore essentially a state of mind, created by perceptions of the past and the present – the past and present of one's own society, and the perceived strength of real or potential rivals? Although perception depends on the angle of vision, there are always likely to be discrepancies between subjective views and objective realities. The national discourse, for instance, may well revolve around decline even in times of growth, as happened in Britain in the 1960s, when the national economy was growing but at a progressively lower rate than the economies of its leading European competitors.[39]

Decline may be relative or – more rarely – absolute, or some combination of the two. In all three instances, however, the difficulty of measurement is enhanced by the influence of perceptions. Paul Kennedy, in his *The Rise and Fall of Great Powers*, coined the term 'imperial overstretch' to explain what happens when a state's resources are no longer sufficient to meet its multiple commitments, including the commitment to defend its far-flung territories.[40] But the assessment of when that point is reached depends on the decision of the governing class, as it tries to draw a balance between immediate pressures and its long-term aspirations. As I suggested in the sentence in *Imperial Spain* about the Spanish ruling class, which seemed to Anthony Sampson to apply so well to twentieth-century Britain, it is not easy for well-entrenched elites, long accustomed to success, to adapt to new times by jettisoning long-held aspirations and attitudes of mind. Their failure to do so only serves to aggravate the difficulties they face, and so to deepen the psychosis of decline.

In spite of that phrase, I was not as aware at the time of writing as I later became of the constant interplay between perception and 'reality', both in the past and the present, that gives the concept of decline its complexity and makes it so difficult for historians to handle. *Imperial Spain* was written within the conventional historical framework of the rise and fall of states and empires, even if the treatment may have appeared unconventional to Spanish readers unfamiliar with recent European trends in historical writing. The fact that the framework was conventional, however, does not necessarily make it invalid. Spain's seventeenth-century 'decline' may be dismissed by some modern historians as a 'myth',[41] but there are several indications that the economy of Castile was less buoyant than it had been in the preceding century,[42] and it is undeniable that, for a variety of reasons, the country did not enjoy the international power and prestige at the end of the seventeenth century that it had enjoyed at its start.

Yet there are alternative ways of approaching the history of Spain and its overseas empire, although I passed lightly over the history of that empire in a book where constraints on space led me to concentrate primarily on Spain itself, and it was only later that I began to engage seriously with the history of its transatlantic possessions.[43] The transformation of Spain since its transition to democracy in the years after 1975 has profoundly influenced the way in which a new generation of Spanish historians see and write the history of their country. Their response to changes in their own society shows that countries in the grip of a psychosis of decline are not necessarily condemned to it for all eternity. As a result of changing attitudes the seventeenth-century tribulations of Spain and the Spanish Monarchy are no longer being automatically set within a framework of decline. Even the history of the second half of the century – conventionally regarded as marking the low-point of decline – is now being recast as a story of resilience in the face of adverse circumstances.[44]

While, then, the narrative of decline has been dominant in the history of states and empires, as it was for seventeenth-century Spaniards and twentieth-century Britons, it need not be the only one. Gibbon himself wrote of Rome that 'the story of its ruin is simple and obvious; and instead of inquiring why the Roman Empire was destroyed, we should rather be surprised that it had subsisted so long'.[45] Survival, however, makes for a different and less spectacular story. Like so many historians before and after him, Gibbon preferred to tell the more dramatic and more historically freighted story of decline and fall.

CHAPTER FIVE

Art and cultural history

Spain's century of 'decline' was also the Golden Age of its arts. By any standards the Spanish seventeenth century was an age of extraordinary cultural creativity, and the artistic achievements and stature of its constellation of artists and writers raise questions of broad historical interest. What relationship, if any, exists between a country's political and economic situation and the vitality, or otherwise, of its cultural life? How far do creative artists simply give expression to the values and preoccupations of the society in which they live, and how far do they actually shape them? Above all, can historians take works of art as a reliable guide to the character of the age or the society that interests them, or are the arts essentially autonomous, moving in response to their own inner rhythms?

As a student of Golden Age Spain I could not escape such questions. Yet in spite of being constantly confronted by them over the years, I cannot claim to have found the answers. No historian can explain the emergence of genius, which by its nature is a random phenomenon, although even genius requires nurturing, and here historical knowledge may be able to contribute something. Talent, however, is another matter, and the conditions that allow talent to flourish, or alternatively that stifle cultural creativity, are a proper subject for historical inquiry. Yet, in an age of increasing specialization, it is not easy for historians to be in command of the many and varied manifestations of creative talent in the societies they are studying. While an obvious point of entry into the history of a society is to soak oneself in the literature and other cultural manifestations of the age, the history of art, literature and music have all developed their own methods, traditions and vocabulary, and it takes time and effort to acquire some familiarity with them. The effort, however, can be a source of intellectual enrichment, in so far as it helps to broaden horizons and break down the artificial barriers that have sprung up between different fields of study.

My own experience in reconstructing the history of the Buen Retiro, the pleasure palace built for Philip IV on the outskirts of Madrid in the 1630s, may perhaps help to suggest something both of the opportunities and of the difficulties that arise from venturing into relatively unfamiliar territory.[1] Although Velázquez's portrait of the Count-Duke of Olivares in the Prado had inspired my original interest in him, and I was already instinctively placing paintings in their historical context by the time I first saw it, I had no particular knowledge of, or expertise in, the history of art, even if Nikolaus Pevsner's lectures had fired my interest in the subject during my days as a Cambridge undergraduate. The more I saw of seventeenth-century European works of art, however, and especially those produced by Spanish artists, the more I felt that they could bring me closer to the age, and the society, that interested me. Inevitably the portraits of the king, his principal minister and other prominent personalities had a particularly strong impact, but visual images, sculptures and buildings all helped to awaken the imagination and strengthen the feeling for period and place. This naturally made me anxious to use them to reconstruct the history of the Spain of Olivares.

It was not simple, however, to see how best to do this, and I was uneasily aware of my lack of art-historical knowledge and expertise. It was a piece of extraordinary good fortune that Jonathan Brown, who was already acquiring an international reputation as a specialist in the history of Spanish Golden Age art, should have been a close neighbour in Princeton. Our mutual interest in seventeenth-century Spain brought us together, and, as we talked, we began to appreciate how each could help, and learn from, the other. The art historian felt the need for more knowledge of the historical background; the political and social historian felt the need for more knowledge of art.

These concerns were hardly surprising, given the changes and challenges that both our disciplines were experiencing in the 1960s and 1970s. Political and social history had been transformed by the aspiration after 'total history' inspired by the *Annales* school, and by this time they were also being heavily influenced by the turn to cultural history. Art history, for its part, was moving away from its traditional preoccupation with questions of connoisseurship and iconography to embrace a broader and more contextual approach, as exemplified by Millard Meiss's *Painting in Florence and Siena after the Black Death*, published in 1951.[2] This pointed to a convergence in the interests of historians and art historians, who were now seeking, in Jonathan Brown's words, to 'place a work of art in the historical-ideological frame of reference in which it was created and to reveal the way in which it expresses ideas in the compressed, charged language of artistic style'.[3]

Having discovered common ground, we began to discuss ways in which we might make common cause. Our first thought was to take a single iconic painting, Velázquez's *Surrender of Breda*, painted in 1634–5, and consider it both as a work of art and as a historical record of the surrender by the Dutch, ten years earlier, of the city of Breda to Ambrosio Spínola, the commander of the Spanish army of Flanders (Plate 6). But it soon became obvious that Velázquez's painting required a still wider contextual approach if its character and purpose were to be fully understood. It was painted at a particular time for a particular place – the Hall of Realms, the central hall of the new palace of the Buen Retiro, then under construction. This suggested the need to be more ambitious: to attempt the 'total history' not just of a painting, but of an entire palace complex.

As a result, we found ourselves embarked on a large-scale collaborative enterprise that would engage us in the constant discussion and exchange of ideas and information over a number of years, would involve our working together in the same archives, and would require, once the task of writing began, the reading and, where necessary, the revision by one author of what the other had written. Because of the growth of specialist fields and subfields and the massive increase in the secondary literature in every field, it seems likely that in the future the writing of history will come to depend heavily on collaborative efforts of this kind. Their most obvious advantage lies in the ability of the participants to tap into each other's area of special expertise; their most obvious disadvantage lies in the difficulty of bringing coherence to the finished product. The work of joint authors can never quite achieve the unified effect, in terms both of approach and of style, of a work by a single author in full command of his or her material. However great their mutual trust, however strong their commitment to speaking with a single voice, there will always be some tension that leaves its traces on the printed page. This is not necessarily to the detriment of the final result, and in some ways it may give the work an extra edge. It is, however, a risk of which joint authors need to be continuously aware. Even if they cannot entirely conjure it away, they do at least have the recompense of knowing that their collaboration has achieved something that it would have been impossible for them to achieve on their own.

At its best, collaboration is a joint learning project, which expands the historical boundaries and imagination of those who take part, and, in the process, can lead to an innovative approach. Because of our respective backgrounds and interests, which, although different, converged in a mutual fascination with Golden Age Spain, we saw the opportunities that might arise from exploring the palace of the Buen Retiro from a variety of viewpoints, and from treating its history in the round. Traditionally the study of palaces has primarily been a topic for architectural historians writing to a restricted brief, although important exceptions exist, like Per Palme's account of James I's intentions in building the Whitehall Banqueting House, which served as a valuable source of inspiration.[4] A purely architectural approach, for which neither of us was fully equipped, would be inadequate to answer the questions that we wanted to ask. We needed to range much wider than this.

We needed, first of all, to discover why Olivares should have decided to build, at great expense, a new palace for a king who already possessed several palaces or country retreats. This required a knowledge of the political history of the period, which my own previous researches, and the political biography of Olivares on which I was engaged, enabled me to provide. I had not, however, paid a great deal of attention to the Count-Duke's cultural programme, which proved to be closely related to his conception of what a King of Spain should be. It became clear that he envisaged his monarch as a ruler who should be supreme in the arts of peace as well as war. This led us into areas that required the expertise of the art historian: the aesthetic and cultural interests of Philip IV, his activities as a collector of works of art, his patronage of artists and men of letters, and his relationship with Velázquez, the supreme artist of the reign. We then needed to look into the plans for building the new palace, the way in which the building operations were organized, the sources of its financing, and the stages of its construction and of the laying out of the surrounding grounds and gardens – subjects that took us into economic, administrative and financial history, as well as the history of architecture and gardens. Once the palace was built, or largely built, it had to be decorated, and we then found ourselves following the complex but fascinating story of the commissioning and acquisition over a few short years in the 1630s of an enormous number of furnishings, paintings and other works of art that would make it a palace worthy of its owner. The palace, however, was more than a mere decorated shell. It was also a building in which people took up residence, and to which they came as visitors and for court diversions. We needed to know how often the king himself used it, and for what purposes. The search for an answer led us into an exploration of court life and festivities, court theatre, and thence into the general theme of the political and social implications of royal expenditure on palace building and court entertainments in a time of war and hardship.

In this sense we found ourselves attempting what was in effect a 'total history', but one which seemed of manageable proportions and was restricted to a relatively short historical period. But we were faced from the outset with what might be regarded as an almost insuperable obstacle: the palace no longer stands, having been largely destroyed by bombardment in the course of the Napoleonic Wars. Since the bombardment was conducted by British forces under the command of General Pakenham, a distant kinsman of my wife, the reconstruction of the palace, if only on paper, might perhaps be regarded as an act of reparation.

By the middle of the nineteenth century only two buildings belonging to the original palace were still standing – the ballroom, known as the Casón, and the great central hall of the palace, the Salón de Reinos, or Hall of Realms, which was converted into a military museum in the nineteenth century. This would not, then, be like writing the history of the Escorial, of which a comprehensive building history would in fact be produced two years after the publication of our book.[5] As our future publisher asked when we first approached him, 'Who will be interested in the history of a palace that no longer exists?'

If we did not have the evidence of the building itself, neither, as it turned out, did we have much in the way of visual images. There was one painting depicting the entire palace complex, made shortly before its completion (Plate 7), and one or two works which showed at least portions of the facade; but no paintings or engravings ever seem to have been made of the interior. We therefore had no visual representation that would allow us to explore its layout and contemplate its decorations and furnishings. This left us largely dependent on written records, and these took a variety of forms. There were financial and administrative records, themselves dispersed through a number of state and notarial archives, which made it possible to follow the various phases of the construction process, and keep track of the expenses incurred by various royal ministers and officials. There was diplomatic correspondence, consisting of letters from foreign ambassadors and other foreign agents in Madrid, reporting home on the progress of the building and its decoration, and on the court activities held in the palace and its gardens. The secretary of the Tuscan ambassador in particular sent frequent and informative letters to his ducal master in Medici Florence, whose cultural ties with Spain were traditionally close. There were also a number of contemporary eyewitness accounts and descriptions, some of them written in verse, and most of them intended to lavish praise on the king and his minister. Finally, we could use the published inventory of the palace's contents, drawn up at the start of the eighteenth century, to reconstruct the layout and discover what paintings adorned the walls of its various rooms and galleries, although only some sixty years after the palace's inauguration.

Historians are programmed to think primarily in terms of written sources, and sufficient written sources survived to make possible a plausible reconstruction of the Retiro's early history, even though they were widely scattered through Spanish and other archives, and were often frustratingly fragmentary. Art and architectural historians, on the other hand, are trained to start with images and artefacts, and use them as the basis for their interpretations. To the historian's instinctive question 'Where are the documents?' the art historian will respond with a different question: 'What can the image tell us?'

It took close and continuing collaboration with an art historian to teach me that an image or object is itself a form of document. Historical evidence is not confined to the written word.

It is true that for centuries historians have made use of images, whether as illustrative background or to add colour to their narratives, but in the nineteenth century their ambitions grew. Hegel's lectures on aesthetics, delivered in Berlin in the 1820s, had a profound impact on the emerging discipline of art history, and, by extension, on the writing of history itself. Jules Michelet and Jacob Burckhardt both absorbed Hegel's belief that art reflected the spirit of a nation and an age, and Hegelian views on the relationship of art to society have continued to influence historians down to our own times. Mannerism, for instance, came to be depicted as the stylistic expression of the spiritual and intellectual crisis of post-Renaissance Europe.[6] The 'Age of the Baroque', as the age of absolute monarchy and a triumphant Roman Catholic Church with global outreach, was seen as intrinsically expressing their ideals, although there was disagreement about how the resulting style was to be interpreted. Some saw baroque art as an art of exuberance, appropriate to an expanding and confident Europe, while others saw it as an art of anxiety and tension, reflecting the turmoils of a seventeenth-century continent in crisis. One of the dangers involved in interpreting 'the spirit of the age' is that historians have a tendency to see the age they are looking for.

As Francis Haskell pointed out in his subtle study *History and its Images*, the validity of an approach to the past through its artefacts is open to question. Huizinga, one of the greatest exponents of this approach, came to recognize this: 'The vision of an epoch resulting from the contemplation of works of art is always incomplete, always too favourable, and therefore fallacious.'[7] There are, as Haskell indicates, several reasons for scepticism, including some that Huizinga himself seems not to have appreciated. The destruction of so many buildings, pictures and images over the course of time is clearly funda-mental – the sheer accident of survival is bound to shape and distort our interpretation of a society when judging it by its visual images or its architectural remains. So too is the changing criterion of beauty, which makes beauty a 'treach-erous guide' for the interpretation of works of an earlier age. Beyond this, however, lie questions about the purposes behind the production of artefacts that are now classed as 'works of art', the conventions that surrounded their creation – for instance, those relating to portraiture – the nature of the patronage that led to their commissioning, and the degree to which the patrons themselves exemplified the interests and values of society at large.[8]

In studying the history and the decoration of a palace that was itself one of the casualties of time, we came up against all these questions in one form or another. For example, among the many paintings commissioned by the crown was a series of twenty-four landscapes with figures of hermits and anchorites, which were painted in Rome by artists of distinction, including Claude and Poussin. Their presence raised significant ques-tions about patronage and purpose – in particular why the king and the coterie around Olivares should have instructed Spain's

1 Diego de Velázquez, *The Count-Duke of Olivares on Horseback*. This portrait of Philip IV's favourite and principal minister, probably painted around 1638, forcefully struck the author on his first visit to the Prado in 1950 and led him to his choice of research subject.

2 The castle archive of Simancas, where the author began his researches in the late summer of 1953. A medieval fortress, from the 1540s onwards it became the repository of the official documents of the Crown of Castile, and it remains to this day one of the greatest of European archives. The photograph shows the main gateway through which researchers would enter the archive in the heat of the afternoon sun on the high plateau of Old Castile.

3 Photograph of the author with the Coderch family of Barcelona, with whom he stayed during his first year of research in Catalonia in 1953–4.

4 Jaume Vicens Vives (standing) and Ferran Soldevila (seated) at a congress held in Sardinia in 1957. Seated behind Vicens are two of his students, Emili Giralt and Jordi Nadal, with whom the author was closely associated during his time in Barcelona.

5 Stephen Farthing, *Historians of 'Past and Present'*. Painted for the National Portrait Gallery in 1999, this group portrait depicts members of the editorial board of the journal in the 1960s, some more recognizable than others (left to right, standing: Eric John Hobsbawm, b. 1917; Rodney Hilton, 1916–2002; Lawrence Stone, 1919–99; Sir Keith Thomas, b. 1933; seated: Christopher Hill, b. 1912; Sir John Elliott, b. 1930; Joan Thirsk, b. 1922). The setting is imaginary but the doorway at the back may have been suggested by Velázquez's *Las meninas*, about which the artist and the author talked as the author sat for him.

6 Diego de Velázquez, *The Surrender of Breda*. Jonathan Brown and the author originally intended to write a short book devoted to Velázquez's iconic work, painted in 1634–5 for the Hall of Realms, the central hall of the palace of the Buen Retiro. It soon became apparent, however, that the painting was best understood if it was firmly placed in the context of the palace for which it was commissioned. This led them to write *A Palace for a King*, first published in 1980.

7 Attributed to Jusepe Leonardo, *Palace of the Buen Retiro*. Painted in 1636–7, while Philip IV's pleasure palace was still under construction, the artist depicts both the palace and the surrounding park and gardens on the eastern outskirts of Madrid. The Hall of Realms, one of only two parts of the palace to survive, is the central wing of the building, with a slate roof tower at either end. Transformed into a military museum in the nineteenth century, the Hall now stands empty, offering possibilities of restoring it to something approaching its appearance in the 1630s.

8 The author and Jonathan Brown at an exhibition, Paintings for the Planet King, held in the Prado Museum in 2005 and aimed at recreating the decorative scheme of the Hall of Realms.

9 Portrait of the author painted by the eminent Spanish artist, Hernán Cortés. The painting, in acrylic, was done in a series of sittings in the artist's studio overlooking the park of the Buen Retiro in the course of the author's visits to Madrid in 2001–2.

agents in Rome to commission a major series of paintings on this distinctive theme. It became clear that the purpose could only be understood in the context of their setting – a gallery that may have been located in the northwestern wing of the palace.

The palace itself began its life as an extension of earlier royal apartments attached to the church and monastery of San Jerónimo, traditionally used by the dynasty for ceremonial occasions and as a place of spiritual and physical retreat, which would give the new palace its name of the 'Retiro'. The idea of retreat was preserved and enhanced during the process of construction by the building of six hermitages, dotted across the palace park and grounds. It was therefore logical to carry the idea of spiritual retreat into the palace itself by commissioning a series of paintings of hermits in landscapes. The resulting commission gave a significant impetus to landscape painting as a genre, particularly in Rome, where it was less practised than in northern Europe.[9] While much still remains to be discovered about where the idea for the series originated, the identity of those responsible for the commissioning, and exactly which artists were involved,[10] the contextualization of these paintings has helped to shed new light on the history of an important pictorial genre, while at the same time emphasizing once again the significance of patronage in directing and shaping the work of artists.

Because it links artistic creation with social aspirations and tendencies, the study of patronage is an obvious area in which historians and art historians can join forces to mutual benefit, and it is well attuned to the interests of an age that has sought to widen the terms of reference in its approach to the past. It is not, therefore, surprising that Francis Haskell's pioneering study *Patrons and Painters* should have had such an impact on the work of historians and art historians alike.[11] Haskell, however, was well aware that the story of the relations between patrons and painters was far from straightforward. 'Inevitably,' he writes in the preface to his book, 'I have been forced to think again and again about the relations between art and society, but nothing in my researches has convinced me of the existence of underlying laws which will be valid in all circumstances. At times the connections between economic or political conditions and a certain style have seemed particularly close; at other times I have been unable to detect anything more than the internal logic of artistic development, personal whim or the workings of chance.'[12]

This is a salutary reminder, not only that conditions vary from place to place and from patron to patron and painter to painter, but also that they vary over time. In another highly influential book, which has had an impact well beyond the world of art historians, Michael Baxandall, in discussing the creation of works of art in fifteenth-century Italy, argues that 'in the fifteenth century painting was still too important to be left to the painters'.[13] This, however, may be less true of the seventeenth century, in which painters were working with some success to break away from the lowly status of the artisan and to insist on the creative gifts of the artist whose skills and inventiveness made him worthy of an enhanced social status.

In the post-Romantic era, when the artist as self-proclaimed genius was expected to follow his muse and felt able as a result to dictate his own terms and conditions, it largely ceased to apply in the realm of painting, although architects, because of the high costs of building, would continue to be heavily dependent on patrons and commissions.

Patronage, therefore, has its limitations as an explanation of the elite cultural manifestations of the nineteenth and twentieth centuries, but in early modern Europe artists and writers operated within a number of constraints, one of the strongest of which lay in the requirements of patrons – a constraint that would hold good as long as there was little or no public market for works of art. Although artists could help to suggest the agenda and at times shape it to their own purposes, the images and artefacts created by early modern societies inevitably reflected the tastes, aspirations and resources of those who had the money. This meant on the one hand the church, with its immense reserves of wealth, especially in Roman Catholic societies, and on the other an elite, made up of princes, nobles and courtiers, royal officials and a number of wealthy merchants and financiers.

Art produced for the church reflected its own special devotional and liturgical requirements, but in many instances it also left scope for expressions of popular devotion that did not necessarily conform to strict ecclesiastical norms. The ex-votos hanging in chapels, or the vestments in which sacred images were dressed, may have offended against decorum, but were genuine manifestations of popular taste and piety, which the ecclesiastical authorities were in certain circumstances willing to tolerate, out of respect for religious fervour or out of fear of the adverse response that might follow from their prohibition.[14] Court art, by contrast, was restricted to a tiny elite, and reserved for the enjoyment of a privileged few, who tended to take their cue from the monarch.

Even when ecclesiastical patronage, speaking to a far wider audience, is added to the equation, the attempt to deduce the character of a society from the cultural artefacts created in response to the tastes and requirements of privileged patrons remains a dubious enterprise. During the middle and later decades of the twentieth century, however, a functionalist approach found some favour as a means of resolving the problem of the connections between a society and its art. One of the most eloquent and sophisticated exponents of this approach was José Antonio Maravall, whose *Culture of the Baroque* (first published in Spanish in 1975) sought to represent the baroque as a *dirigiste* culture, designed to instil obedience and respect for authority in hierarchically organized societies. Although censorship and repression were part of the story, Maravall argued that the visual arts, literature and the theatre were all vigorously employed to engage the emotions and to move and persuade. Maravall's baroque culture was an activist culture directed from above, and 'all the multiplicity of controls that governed the baroque were centralized in the monarchy'.[15]

Baroque art thus becomes a court art, which, although intrinsically the art of the few, was used by the authorities to overawe and impress the many. This sociological and function-alist approach to baroque culture has obvious similarities with the approach to the history of European courts by the German Jewish refugee Norbert Elias (1897–1990), although there is no indication that Maravall was aware of Elias's work. This is not surprising, since Elias's *The Court Society*, although largely drafted in the 1920s, was not published until 1969 (in German), and it was only in the concluding decades of the century that, after a slow beginning, this work and the same author's *The Civilizing Process* brought Elias belated international fame.[16]

The court, as depicted by Elias, was the institution that enabled European monarchs over the centuries to domesticate and civilize their nobilities through the inculcation of chivalric and courtly behaviour. By establishing the exact precedence of each individual in an elaborately structured hierarchy of rank and status, the ceremonial and etiquette imposed by the monarch were the instruments by means of which he set his nobles against each other while binding them to himself. The system, as Elias presents it, reached its apogee at the court of Louis XIV, whose absolutist model set the standard for other European courts. Although at many points highly suggestive, Elias's work has been criticized on a number of counts. His model, even as a representation of the court of Louis XIV, is too crude and mechanistic. It fails, too, to take into account the important differences of structure and ceremonial between European courts, especially those of Bourbon France and the Habsburg courts of Madrid and Vienna. Moreover, it rests on a concept of absolutism that now appears dated. The relationship between monarchs and their aristocracies, conducted within a framework of ceremonial in which both parties were to some extent prisoners, depended throughout the early modern period not so much on royal *fiat* as on a willingness to accept the monarch as role model in matters of culture, taste and social comportment. In the world of politics, it depended on continuous if not always explicit 'negotiation' or bargaining rather than on the forcible imposition of the royal will.[17]

Elias's functionalist and sociological approach, although influential, never in fact succeeded in dominating the field of court studies. These developed their own momentum, and tended to be more influenced by symbolic anthropologists like Clifford Geertz than by a functionalism that was already beginning to look outmoded when Elias's work was finally published. The unusual publication history of Elias's *Court Society*, coupled with the rapidly developing interest in symbolic anthropology, helps to explain why a wide-ranging survey of European courts between 1400 and 1800 published in 1977 managed to ignore Elias's contribution entirely.[18]

Court studies were also profoundly influenced by the remarkable scholarship of Frances Yates (1899–1981), who demonstrated in *The Valois Tapestries* (1959) and subsequent works how European princes commissioned works of art and organized court festivals in order to make political statements and convey political messages. It was by means of a magnificent set of tapestries designed and produced at the instigation of

William of Orange that the leader of the Dutch revolt against the Spain of Philip II sought to encourage the House of Valois to come to the help of the Netherlands in its struggle for independence.[19] The lasting achievement of Frances Yates and of those who have followed her lead has been to reveal the central role of the image in the life and thought of early modern Europe, and the resulting closeness of the relationship between art and power. In the brilliant imagery of court festivals princely power expressed itself as art – art that, by insisting on the resolution of conflict and the representation of harmony, stood in for power and ideally would enhance it, by giving spectators a glimpse of the world not as it was but as it was supposed to be in the imaginings of those who governed it. Truth, it was assumed, could be learned through images. Emblems and allegorical depictions served as clues to the deeper realities of an unseen and harmonious world.[20]

Yates's imaginative interweaving of themes drawn from the standard fields of political history, intellectual history and the history of art suggests how much is to be gained from an integrated approach. Courts and court society, with their rich written records and the survival of so many objects designed for court purposes, have provided an especially favourable setting for such an approach. The context of the court can help, for example, to illuminate the history of European portraiture, while simultaneously enriching the study of political history.[21] As a court artist Velázquez operated within a tradition of Spanish royal portraiture that eschewed allegory, and was deliberately understated. If this tells us something about why

Velázquez painted royal portraits as he did, it also tells us something about Spanish attitudes to kingship. The greatest monarch in the world had no need to resort to ostentatious imagery to impress that world with his power and majesty. The Medici Grand Dukes of Tuscany might seek to assert and enhance their status with the help of allegorical representations and illusionistic skills, but a Spanish Habsburg had no need to resort to such artificial devices. A sober and lifelike representation of the monarch was sufficient of itself to create in the spectator a proper sense of reverence and awe.[22]

In recent years a number of exhibitions in museums and galleries have shown how much the understanding and appreciation of paintings and other works of art can be deepened by displaying them within the context of the court or ecclesiastical culture that gave rise to their creation. In 2002, for instance, Jonathan Brown and I curated for the Prado Museum an exhibition designed to illustrate the political, artistic and cultural relations between Spain and Great Britain during the first half of the seventeenth century. On opposing walls were placed the portraits of the principal political figures of the age, notably Philip IV of Spain and Charles I of England, who, as Prince of Wales, travelled incognito to Madrid in 1623 to press his suit in person for the hand of Philip's sister, the Infanta Doña María. The exhibition, appropriately inaugurated by their modern descendants, Charles, Prince of Wales, and Philip, Prince of Asturias, went on to demonstrate the impact of that visit on subsequent artistic relations between the English and Spanish courts, as the two monarchs refined their aesthetic sensibilities in its aftermath, and competed for masterpieces that would enhance their collections. The display reached its climax in the years immediately following the execution of Charles I in 1649, when the 'sale of the late king's goods' allowed the Spanish ambassador in London to secure surreptitiously for his royal master leading works from Charles's collection, including Titian's great portrait of the Emperor Charles V with a hound, which Philip had over-generously presented to the prince in 1623.[23]

An exhibition of this kind, displaying and publishing important documents and placing works of art in a close historical context, suggests how fruitful the marriage of history, art history and museum curatorship can be.[24] The contextualization of works of art within the court culture for which they were created has undoubtedly done much to revitalize interest in the history of collectors and collecting by raising questions of social and cultural history that extend beyond the more traditional themes of taste and connoisseurship.[25] It has helped, too, to focus attention on artefacts traditionally classified as belonging to the minor arts. In the art historical canon, painting has long enjoyed a privileged position. As we became aware, however, in examining the acquisition of art objects for the Buen Retiro, this did not reflect contemporary priorities. Although by the seventeenth century some living painters, like Rubens, could command high prices, and a number of their sixteenth-century predecessors, like Titian, were being admitted into a developing category of 'old masters' whose works were eagerly sought after, the price of easel paintings could not compare with that of tapestries or pieces of ornate furniture, which required expensive materials and high levels of craftsmanship. A richly ornamented cabinet presented to Philip IV was valued at 30,000 ducats and a single tapestry might cost 5,000 or 6,000 or more, but it is rare to find a painting that cost above 500 or 600 ducats.[26] The prices paid for luxury objects tell a story of their own about contemporary valuations of the various art forms, and thus serve as useful guides to fluctuations in style and taste.

Questions of craftsmanship and provenance deserve study in their own right, but they also have social, political and cultural implications that should not be neglected. Our attempt to trace the processes by which works of art were acquired for the Buen Retiro underlines with startling clarity the enormous importance of gift-giving in the assembling of personal collections and the adornment of royal or aristocratic residences. This is hardly surprising. Following the trail blazed in the 1920s by Marcel Mauss in his study *The Gift*, anthropologists have paid close attention to the exchange of gifts as a device for the establishment and perpetuation of social cohesion.[27] Historians of early modern European societies have been rather slower to examine the process, partly perhaps because of Mauss's own assumption that gift-giving as a form of reciprocal exchange diminished over time, and tended to be replaced by gift-giving as a unilateral act.[28] Yet gifts of rich hangings, ornate furniture and valuable paintings, whether presented by his own subjects or by foreign rulers, were crucial to the adornment of Philip IV's new palace. The tracing of such gifts –

some more voluntary than others – can shed a flood of light on the provenance of paintings that are now to be found in the great national museums. Equally, it can be used to reveal the character and strength of the relationship between donor and recipient, and not least between one prince and another in a period when works of art came to be regarded as important signifiers of mutual respect, gratitude or subservience in the world of international diplomacy.[29]

The splendidly adorned interior of the Retiro palace, with its profusion of tapestries and paintings, raises a question central to the history of European courts: the motivation behind princely ostentation and display. It has become standard practice to describe court art and architecture, and court ritual and festivities, as conveying a series of 'messages'. But there are messages and messages, just as there are also audiences and audiences, and it is important to discover what was intended, and for whom. In societies where conspicuous consumption was a mark of social status, display was expected of those at the top of the social pyramid, and of monarchs most of all. The interior of the Buen Retiro was appropriately spectacular, and clearly impressed the relatively few – courtiers, diplomats and privileged visitors – who were granted access. The exterior was criticized as being unworthy of a great monarch to the extent that some consideration was given to making it more majestic, but this was a palace designed for private enjoyment rather than for affairs of state.

This in itself tempered any message of princely grandeur for the world to admire. In addition, however, monarchs in times of war and economic hardship had to draw a careful line between the *liberalitas* that was expected of them, and *prudentia* in the expenditure of money on royal extravagances. In the Buen Retiro, and partly in response to criticisms of royal wastefulness, the central Hall of Realms, designed for court festivities and theatrical performances, was also appropriated for state occasions, and given a decorative scheme that served to emphasize its importance as a political space. This scheme, consisting of specially commissioned paintings depicting the monarch and his immediate family and a series of victories won during the course of his reign, was designed to impress those who entered the hall with the power of the monarch and the glory of his dynasty.

This was a generalized message of monarchical power of the kind that is to be expected in royal palaces. Informed observers, however, are also likely to have picked up a number of more specific messages. The depiction of twelve victories won since the accession of Philip to the throne was a reminder not only of Spain's continuing military might at a time when the regime's domestic and foreign policies were being subjected to strong criticism, but also of the wise management of affairs by the monarch and his principal minister as they sought to sustain and defend a worldwide Monarchy. As for Velázquez's *Surrender of Breda*, it provided the perfect visual image of the magnanimity to be expected of a King of Spain in the hour of victory.[30]

But for whom were the messages intended? In our own age, dominated as it is by the media, the natural tendency is to think in terms of propaganda, but the self-representation of princes and their governments in the early modern era is better understood as a manifestation of the obsessive contemporary concern with reputation. The paintings in the Hall of Realms were seen by relatively few people, and it is to be assumed that many, if by no means all, of those who viewed them were sympathetic to the aspirations, claims and intentions of the regime that had commissioned them. For them the paintings were no more than the visual affirmation of the reputation to which the regime laid claim through its actions. But reputation was not simply a matter of contemporary responses. Life was brief but fame was eternal, and visual imagery would inform future generations of the glorious accomplishments of those who had preceded them. Over and above any immediate political value that it may have possessed, the iconographic programme of the Hall of Realms performed the same function as Rubens's cycle of paintings in the Palais du Luxembourg narrating the turbulent life of Marie de Médicis, or his depiction in the Whitehall Banqueting House of the benefits that James I conferred on his kingdoms through his wise and beneficent rule. Its principal aim was to ensure the eternal renown of the figures it commemorated.[31]

The political danger of such forms of representation is that a regime begins to believe what it says about itself. Monarchical power can all too easily fall victim to its own self-glorification; and, as the fate of Charles I suggests, the idealized world of the court masque, culminating in the harmonious resolution of conflict, is incapable of replacing the untidier world outside, or of permanently preventing it from forcing its way through the palace gates. All regimes, however, have an outward- as well as an inward-looking face. The very attempt of a regime to legitimize itself and its actions before the world at large presupposes the existence of some form of public opinion capable of being moulded and manipulated to serve its purposes. Although much has been made of Habermas's assumption that a 'public sphere' emerged only in the eighteenth century, there can be no doubting the existence of at least an embryonic public opinion in the societies of early modern Europe, and regimes made use of such devices as were available to them to justify their behaviour and promote their aims.

These devices included not only the written word in a variety of forms, both popular and learned, but also visual imagery making use of woodcuts and engravings and royal portraits prominently displayed. The mass mobilization of a population, however, was beyond the technical capacity of early modern states, and it was by means of public celebrations and royal progresses, like those undertaken through France by Catherine de Médicis or through England by Elizabeth I, that monarchs had the best chance of impressing and influencing large numbers of their subjects.

The court itself was not necessarily behind all such public manifestations. The preparation of ceremonial entries into cities, and the commissioning of the festival architecture needed for the occasion, generally fell to the cities themselves. A great city like Antwerp, which commissioned Rubens to design the magnificent street decorations for the ceremonial entry in 1634 of Philip IV's brother, the Cardinal-Infante Ferdinand, hoped to impress on the royal visitor, by way of the images and symbols displayed along his route, the importance of the city and the loyalty of its citizens, while also seeking to convey specific municipal concerns.[32] Such representations are likely to tell us more about the city than about the prince, and in this respect ceremonial entries and other festivities could well become 'sites of political contestation' in which royal and non-royal messages competed for primacy.[33] Yet where royal events were instigated or stage-managed by the court, they can provide useful clues to a regime's intentions, as well as to its perception of itself. They are less useful, however, as indications of the cultural life and attitudes of a whole society.

These have to be deduced from a wide variety of sources, and cultural history over the past few decades has widened its net under the influence of cultural anthropology to cover numerous activities extending far beyond 'culture' as it was once understood. In contrast to concentration on the high aesthetics of artistic creation, the study of so-called 'popular culture', as an expression of how the mass of the population thought, spoke and behaved, has developed into the major historical growth industry of our times. It has given rise to some remarkable works of 'microhistory' that seek, by recovering the mental and social worlds of a single individual such as the previously unknown miller of Friuli now made famous by the detective work of Carlo Ginzburg, to illuminate popular attitudes, assumptions and beliefs that were thought to be irrecoverable.[34] It has also done much to recover another lost world, that of women, whose lives received a pioneering treatment from Eileen Power in the 1930s,[35] but were still seriously neglected until the 1970s.

A microhistorical searchlight, whether shone on a theologically confused miller or a lesbian nun,[36] can illuminate many dark corners of hidden private worlds. Yet, for all its fascinating revelations of individual life stories, there remains a fundamental dilemma at the heart of microhistory. How far is the individual truly representative of the larger society to which she or he belongs? The very fact that inquisitorial or trial records tend to be the principal source for the reconstruction of such individual lives immediately singles them out from those of the mass of the population who left little or no written trace of their passage through the world. It may be questioned whether individual case studies, however skilfully conducted, can really tell us much of universal import about the 'popular culture' of this silent majority.

While scepticism is in order, it is clear that, in spite of the distortion of much of the evidence through misunderstanding and manipulation as the process shifts from inquisitor to victim and back again to inquisitor, a great deal of unexpected information can in fact be recovered. There is no better proof of this than the results of the massive growth in studies of witchcraft over the past few decades – so massive indeed that it seems at times as if the study of early modern Europe has been reduced to a study of its witches.[37] We now know far more about the place of superstition, magic and the devil in the mental universe of early modern societies than we knew half a century ago.[38] Yet, as historians attempt to construct their ethnographies of attitudes and behaviour, many questions remain, over and above the kinds of difficulties of recovering and interpreting evidence that face all historians, irrespective of their field. What, for instance, are the relative contributions of oral and written tradition to the making of the mental and cultural worlds of early modern – or, for that matter, modern and contemporary – societies? How are we to 'read' the meaning of popular festivals, such as carnival? And, beyond this, is it really possible to draw a line between popular and elite culture in early modern Europe?[39]

The evidence so far suggests that while such a line existed and seems to have grown stronger with the passage of time, it was also highly porous, with different worlds – elite and popular, court and urban, urban and rural – overlapping and interacting with each other, to greater or lesser degrees of intensity, according to time and place. Processions and carnivals, street theatre and firework displays, brought disparate social groups into contact with each other. Companies of players performed in public playhouses but also at court, creating a shared world of language, behaviour and narrative. Yet court culture in particular spoke a language of its own, frequently making use of allegorical allusions and visual imagery that would have been understood only by the cognoscenti. Too much can easily be read into these supposed messages, many of which are likely to have been no more than *jeux d'esprit* for the enjoyment and entertainment of princes, their families and their court circle, and offering a no doubt welcome relief from the tedium of court life. Not all imagery was designed for 'projection', and not every symbol had a solemn meaning.

Even if over-interpretation joins the post-modern insistence on the impossibility of interpretation as one of the sins of our age, the combined work of cultural and art historians has given us valuable insights into concealed or partially concealed features of early modern societies. There have, however, been losses as well as gains. Not everything in life can be reduced to 'representation'. Governments may have deployed imagery to greater or lesser effect, but behind the symbols lay the harsh realities of power. The new cultural and art history can help us to know and understand how images were conceived, produced and received, but the resulting information, however fascinating in itself, can give us only a partial view into the complex social, political and economic life of past societies. Politics is more than 'political culture', just as art is more than a set of symbols and 'messages' that need to be decoded.

The new cultural history, in its laudable desire to embrace all human experience, navigates a difficult course between becoming an amorphous catch-all and privileging what can be no more than a partial vision of the world. The long-term consequence may well be a movement back towards reasserting the autonomous character of a variety of fields of study, whether intellectual history, the history of art, literature and science, or their various subfields. In some respects this would represent a salutary readjustment of the balance, which has tipped too far in favour of social explanations of cultural movements and phenomena. The arts possess their own dynamic – a dynamic born of a response to their own distinctive traditions and creative achievements, over and above the social, intellectual or political environment that gives rise to them. The Hall of Realms, for example, took its place in a long line of European 'halls of princely virtue' – royal and princely galleries built and decorated in conformity with an established set of conventions – and it has to be seen in this context as well as in that of the political and cultural requirements of the moment.[40]

The recovery and understanding of those conventions require specialist knowledge and expertise, which are not gained overnight. Without them, art history, like any other form of history, runs the risk of floating in a relativist sea. This is not, however, to suggest that the time has come for a timid return to the safety of the shore. The days of positivism in art history, or any other form of history, are over. The mere accumulation of facts for facts' sake, and simplistic notions about the 'objective reality' of evidence, have rightly been dismissed as offering inadequate approaches to the study of the past. 'Art in context', in common with 'ideas in context', is here to stay. That context, however, needs to be carefully defined, and attention paid not only to the general characteristics of a society and an age, but also to the specific characteristics and requirements of a particular art form and the ways in which it continually refers back to itself.

The relationship of art to society remains as elusive as ever, but the study of images and objects has opened doors on the past that were previously closed. It has given us new insights into the values and priorities of societies, or at least of particular sections of them, and into the ways in which works of art may be used for political purposes or for purposes of prestige. Above all, the artistic creations and literature of a society or an age have done more than anything else to define its character in the eyes of future generations. In that sense it is the creative artists who have had the final word.

They must, however, be given the opportunity, wherever possible, to have their works displayed as they were intended to be seen, and in this sense our reconstruction of the Buen Retiro remains unfinished business. In *A Palace for a King* we were able to suggest how the Hall of Realms looked at the time of its inauguration, and how the three series of paintings commissioned for the hall – five equestrian royal portraits by Velázquez, twelve battle paintings by the leading Spanish artists of the day, and ten depictions by Zurbarán of episodes from the life of Hercules, the mythical founder of Spain's ruling dynasty – may have been arranged around its walls. All but one of those twenty-seven paintings survive and are to be found in the Prado, although not all are on display. Above all, the original structure of the Hall of Realms, for which they were intended, also survives, and stands in the vicinity of the Prado itself.

The survival both of an early modern palace, or at least of its most important feature, and of the paintings or other works of art intended for its decoration is very rare – Inigo Jones's Banqueting House retains its ceiling panels by Rubens but not the tapestries that originally hung on its walls, while Rubens's Marie de Médicis cycle has survived but not the Palais du Luxembourg for which it was designed. Our reconstruction of the decorative scheme of the Hall of Realms suggests that, given the survival in a relatively unchanged form of this seventeenth-century space, it would be possible to restore it to something approaching its original appearance. Since the publication of our book we have campaigned for such a restoration, and the idea has been endorsed in principle both by the Spanish government and by the trustees of the Prado Museum.[41] In 2010, as a result of our campaign, the army museum which had occupied the hall since the mid-nineteenth century was removed to a more appropriate site in the castle of the Alcázar in Toledo, leaving the Hall of Realms an empty shell.

Whether the hall will indeed be restored to appear much as it looked in the days of Velázquez remains an open question, and the future of the project depends both on a willingness to abide by earlier commitments and on the availability of the substantial resources that would be needed for its realization. But, as was made clear by the reassembling of the paintings in a Prado exhibition held in 2005,[42] there is no need to doubt that the results would be both impressive and historically significant (Plate 8). The Hall of Realms was emblematic of the glories of Golden Age Spain, and its restoration would not only represent the spectacular recovery of a splendid seventeenth-century space, but, above all, do what works of art are uniquely equipped to do – bring an age to life.

CHAPTER SIX

Comparative history

A T the Sixth International Congress of Historical Sciences, held in Oslo in 1928, Marc Bloch made an eloquent plea for a comparative history of European societies.[1] He believed that a comparative approach would allow historians, by looking both for similarities and for differences, to identify what, if anything, was unique about the society they were studying. Bloch was in fact by no means the first historian to draw attention to the possibilities inherent in comparative approach. A French predecessor, Charles-Victoire Langlois, made a similar plea in 1890, and the great Belgian historian Henri Pirenne chose the theme of comparative history for his keynote address to the 1923 International Historical Congress in Brussels.[2] Bloch's exposition, however, was more rigorous, and its impact more long-lasting. Yet while historians continue to applaud his lecture, they have seemed reluctant to put the theory into practice. As a result, systematic comparative history remains the Cinderella among approaches to the past.

Since the days of Plutarch historians have drawn parallels and set up comparisons, although not necessarily pursuing them with rigour. During the first half of the twentieth century Otto Hintze, in particular, proved to be a powerful comparative historian. Although the large-scale comparative history of constitutional and administrative developments on which he embarked never saw the light of day, his articles comparing European state structures and representative institutions revealed him as a historian fully conscious of the possibilities inherent in comparative history, even if he did not theorize about it at length. He did, however, draw a distinction between the approach of the historian and that of the sociologist: 'You can compare in order to find something general that underlies the things that are compared, and you can compare in order to grasp more clearly the singularity of the thing that is compared, and to distinguish it from the others. The sociologist does the former, the historian, the latter.'[3]

In reality, Hintze himself blurred this dividing line in his own work, as when, influenced by the work of Max Weber, he posited an ideal type of feudalism and used it to assess the degree to which patterns of social relationships in Europe, Asia and the Islamic world conformed to the ideal. It was, however, social scientists, and those historians who felt most strongly the influence of the social sciences such as Marc Bloch and Fernand Braudel, who made the running in exploiting a comparative approach during much of the twentieth century.

This is not surprising. There is a long and distinguished comparativist tradition among practitioners of what may loosely be described as the social sciences, reaching all the way back, through Montesquieu and Vico, to Herodotus himself. It was, however, in the nineteenth century that the comparative method began to establish itself in a variety of disciplines: comparative philology with Franz Bopp; comparative religion with Max Müller; comparative jurisprudence with Sir Henry Maine; comparative anthropology with Sir James Frazer. Twentieth-century social scientists built on this long comparative tradition, leaving historians to follow in the rear.

Various possible explanations have been adduced for the lack of enthusiasm displayed by historians over much of the twentieth century for the comparative method.[4] Many of them practised a narrative history that was short on analysis, and comparative history requires an analytical approach. Historians, too, are programmed by their training to focus on the unique circumstance or event, and instinctively tend to be sceptical of anything that speaks of general laws. Every general law propounded by a social scientist somehow has a way of bumping up against an inconvenient fact. Consequently, historians are reluctant to embark on attempts at comparison until they have succeeded in corralling what appear to be all the relevant facts. Since this takes time, the process of synthesizing can be endlessly prolonged. Once a satisfactory synthesis is achieved, it is still necessary, for purposes of comparison, to identify an area or a period for which a roughly similar level of synthesis makes the exercise feasible. In the circumstances, it is understandable that all too often the game does not seem worth the candle.

In turning their backs on a comparative approach, however, historians are prone to overlook the awkward fact that more or less concealed comparisons lurk in many of their own pronouncements. Let us take an imaginary pronouncement, of the kind that is so common in historical literature: 'The English throughout their history have shown a genius for political compromise.' Effectively this asserts that the English have been more successful in avoiding domestic conflict than their continental neighbours – most obviously the French. But this is an assertion, not a demonstration, and effective demonstration would demand explicit comparison with at least one continental society, and ideally with more.

It is perhaps easier for historians working on topics in foreign rather than their own native history to recognize the need to think comparatively. In working on Spanish history, and especially when writing *Imperial Spain*, I found myself relating it time after time to the history of Britain and Europe. Which Spanish developments were unique, and which had parallels in contemporary societies? Was the Spanish obsession with honour, for example, an exclusively Spanish phenomenon? If not, where else was it to be found, and was the Spanish sense of honour different in character or intensity from that found in other societies, and especially in those of the Mediterranean world, where it has received extensive study?[5] Even if I did not specifically set out to answer such questions, they lurked in the background of my thinking every time I was confronted with honour-related matters in early modern Spain. I was made all the more aware of them because of the need to make the history of Spain accessible to a non-Hispanic readership, and the choice of familiar points of reference is always a useful device for those engaged in writing about unfamiliar societies.

Implicit comparisons, of the kind continually made by historians, are one thing. Explicit comparisons are another, and it is here that historians have been content to let social scientists, some of them with a strong historical bent, make the running. State formation, revolution and the origins of capitalism all lend themselves to a large-scale comparative approach, and social scientists and sociologically minded historians have seized the opportunity, sometimes with impressive results. Barrington Moore's *Social Origins of Dictatorship and Democracy*, for instance, ranges across countries and continents, and has been widely praised for the imaginative boldness of its attempt to trace and explain the ways in which differing power relationships in a variety of agrarian societies led to different forms of political organization in different parts of the industrialized world.[6]

Revolutions, in particular, offer rich opportunities for comparison, and, in examining the causes of revolts and revolutions in the Europe of the 1640s, the contributors to the great debate of the 1950s and 1960s on the General Crisis of the seventeenth century were engaged in a comparative exercise, if of a rather unsystematic character.[7] The very attempt to divide revolts and revolutions into categories requires a degree of comparison,[8] but it is sociologists rather than historians who have been boldest in the development of systematic comparison across time and space. The impulse behind their comparative work comes from the desire to develop widely applicable theories of revolution, but they vary in the degree to which they are theory-led. Historians are likely to feel less comfortable with works that use case histories to confirm and illustrate some all-embracing theory or theories, like S. N. Eisenstadt's *The Political Systems of Empires*, than with more contextualized explorations, like those conducted by Charles Tilly or Theda Skocpol, which help to explain historical developments as they seek to establish some general principles.[9]

Authors of works of 'macro-analytical' comparative history, as it has been called,[10] have no hesitation in comparing societies as different as Skocpol's societies of choice – those of the France of 1789, the Russia of 1917, and twentieth-century China. Time- and space-bound historians may feel uneasy about such broad-based comparisons, but there is no good reason why comparison should not be made between sharply differing societies, or those of different ages, as long as the purpose of the comparison is clearly stated. A comparative approach is no more than one useful device among many for the solving of problems, and the nature of the problem should be allowed to determine the nature of the comparison. Social scientists or historians who may be interested in the decline of empires as a general problem will obviously have recourse to evidence from as many empires as they can muster. If, on the other hand, their concern is with the decline of one specific empire, such as that of Spain, and they suspect that certain patterns tend to repeat themselves in the process of imperial decline, the Roman Empire offers a more useful unit of comparison than the Chinese, since – as Spaniards themselves were well aware – Spain's empire took its place in a western tradition of empire that stretched back to imperial Rome. Yet a Spanish–Roman comparison by no means rules out a comparison with the Chinese empire when it seems that this might be helpful. For all the remoteness of China, it might still provide a useful controlling element, since its inclusion in the comparison can focus attention on some aspect of the process of decline that might otherwise escape notice – for example, the obstructive role of bureaucracy in preventing reforms essential for imperial survival.

This suggests that, as Marc Bloch recognized, comparison can be used for a variety of purposes. At its most modest it can be used for purposes of illustration. If we are told, for instance, that Charles I lacked regular forms of taxation, like the *taille* in France and the *millones* in Spain,[11] this can illuminate his predicament, but does not seek to explain how a King of England came to find himself in it. Illustrative comparisons of this kind are a stock-in-trade of all historians, but, however suggestive, they hardly rank as genuine comparative history, which moves beyond illustration into explanation and analysis.

Beyond the modest illustrative comparison at one end of the spectrum and the macro-analytical comparison at the other, there lies a middle ground of comparison of the kind that Marc Bloch seems to have been advocating. 'The comparative method', he wrote, 'can do much ... But it cannot do every-thing: in science, there is no talisman.'[12] For Bloch the compar-ative method was a form of hypothesis-testing.[13] It enabled historians to test explanatory hypotheses about one society by looking for the presence or absence of what appeared to be its distinguishing characteristics in other contemporary societies. It could also lead to the discovery of new historical facts, particularly where the evidence for the existence of some historical phenomenon was clearer or more abundant for one society than for another, for which less documentation was available. Comparison could help, too, to identify common causes underlying social, political or economic developments in different states and societies, and could assist in the detection of mutual influences. But above all, he saw comparative history as a device for widening the horizons of historians, with their natural tendency to focus on the particular. 'Comparative studies', as he put it, 'are alone capable of dissipating the mirage of false local causes.'[14]

It is, however, one thing, as Bloch himself was well aware, to proclaim the virtues of a comparative approach, and another to practise it. The most immediate and pressing question is the choice of the units for comparison. Fernand Braudel, in his last book, *L'identité de la France*, put the case for comparative history as 'a history that seeks to compare like with like – the condition of all social science if the truth be told'.[15] But what constitutes 'like'? Societies may be very different and yet have one or more common characteristics, such as the two Islamic societies of Indonesia and Morocco, studied by Clifford Geertz, who saw them as 'offering a kind of commentary on one another's character'.[16] For Geertz it is the contrasts, rather than the likenesses, that are most illuminating, but his comparison would lose its point if the two societies did not enjoy the commonality of a shared religion.

The identification of contrasts as well as of similarities is integral to the practice of comparative history, but there is bound to be a question about the degree to which the exercise is worth the effort when the contrasts appear so wide as to be unbridgeable. Can apples and oranges usefully be compared? They may be incomparable where matters of taste are concerned, but nevertheless there are obvious points of comparison when it comes to examining their relative nutritional value, or the methods and costs of production. This would give some point to their comparison, whereas there is little to be gained from a comparison of apples and electric light bulbs, even if there may be rough similarities of size, shape and weight. The choice of the units of comparison would therefore seem to be best determined by the nature of the question to be asked, and by the degree to which even a rough or superficial similarity is likely to yield interesting facts or raise suggestive hypotheses.

In practice a persistent tension between similarity and difference lies at the heart of the comparative enterprise, and it is best that this tension should be frankly acknowledged, and seen for what it is: as an opportunity for creative possibilities within some clear constraints, as Clifford Geertz appreciated when comparing Morocco with Indonesia. A recognition of those constraints demands a degree of modesty of the kind inherent in Marc Bloch's approach to comparative history as a device for testing whether the local does indeed have a wider resonance, or whether the general can shed light on the particular. The results of the comparison, however, may not themselves be modest.

The historical problem of attitudes to poverty in sixteenth-century Europe offers a useful illustration. With the massive rise in population, and growing disparities in wealth between the rich and the poor, central and municipal governments across Europe were faced with major problems of vagrancy and public disorder. Late nineteenth- and early twentieth-century British historians did some impressive work on the responses of Tudor England to this challenge – responses that combined imaginative welfare schemes with some highly repressive social legislation. These historians were well aware that other sixteenth-century European states were also legislating to tackle the problem of poverty and social dislocation. Out of this awareness there emerged the influential thesis that a sharp distinction existed between the attitudes to poverty of Protestant societies dominated by a powerful work ethic and those of Roman Catholic societies which regarded alms-giving as an important instrument for the salvation of souls. A later generation of historians, including one of my own students, Brian Pullan, working on sixteenth-century Venice, looked more closely at practice as well as theory in Catholic Europe, and concluded that there were more similarities than contrasts in the attitudes of Protestant and Catholic societies to problems of poor relief.[17] This, however, still left important differences that had to be accounted for, and Paul Slack went on to identify significant contrasts between English and French responses to poverty, for which he advanced some tentative explanations, including the relative absence in England both of large cities and of provincial autonomy.[18]

This example suggests how historical understanding can be advanced by the making and refining of comparisons. In the process we can hope both to banish misconceptions and to identify new questions for research. Once the units of comparison have been chosen, however, another difficulty presents itself. How is a level playing field to be achieved? It is highly implausible that the societies or events to be compared will be equally well documented, and, even where the documentation of the two or more units of comparison is rich, it will not necessarily have been exploited by historians in the same way or to the same degree. This is bound to complicate the task of drawing fair comparisons.

I had direct personal experience of this when embarking on my comparative study of Richelieu and Olivares for the Trevelyan Lectures I gave in Cambridge in 1983.[19] My first thought was to compare the Spain of Olivares and the France of Richelieu in an attempt to see why France eventually emerged the victor. Was it a question of larger resources, better military organization, or more effective leadership, or of other, less immediately perceptible considerations, such as geographical situation or political and religious culture? I quickly realized that the state of the historical literature made such a comparison, at least at that moment, an impossibly ambitious enterprise. Compared with the massive literature on seventeenth-century France, the literature on most aspects of the history of Spain in the same century was meagre, and it was clear that there was no way of presenting the Spanish side of the equation in equal depth. It was true that for Spain I could draw to some extent on my own researches, but there was no large secondary literature for me to fall back on to supplement my own investigations. For France, on the other hand, I had no direct archival experience, but much of the information I was likely to require was readily accessible in print. Most comparative historians are likely to find themselves facing this kind of asymmetry, since few are likely to feel equally at home in both, or all, the societies they are studying.

In the circumstances, discretion seemed the better part of valour, and I felt it would be wise to confine my comparison to the figures of the two statesmen who guided the fortunes of their respective countries in the 1620s and 1630s, the two critical decades that opened the way to the eventual triumph of France. This at least seemed a more manageable exercise, and promised a greater degree of coherence. Even then, however, I found myself having to balance ignorance against information, and information against ignorance. Much more is known, for instance, about the nobility of seventeenth-century France than about that of Spain, but rather less about the intricacies of French than of Spanish crown finances.

If comparison consists, as Braudel asserts, in comparing 'like with like', a comparison between Richelieu and Olivares seemed a promising undertaking. Here were two statesmen who were bitter rivals and almost exact contemporaries. Richelieu was born in 1585 and Olivares two years later. Olivares came to power in 1621, Richelieu in 1624, and their tenure of office ended within a few weeks of each other – Richelieu's with his death at the end of 1642, and that of Olivares with his effective dismissal a few weeks later. The similarities, however, did not stop here. Each man was the third son of a noble father who found employment in royal service. But this simple fact suggests one of the problems inherent in comparative history. Are we dealing here with coincidence, or does the similarity point to some wider consideration that is worthy of note? In this instance, the similarity is at least suggestive, in that it highlights the problems of younger sons of noble families who had to make their own way in the world. A common option for a younger son was to make a career in the church, and there was a further similarity in that both Richelieu and Olivares received an education with this in mind, although only Richelieu would follow through with an ecclesiastical career, since the death of Olivares's surviving brother meant that he would become head of the family and hence was expected to marry and perpetuate the line.

While in this case there was an initial coincidence, the co-incidence went on to create a number of similarities, not least in the educational background of the two men. Training for the church had implications for their cultural outlook and their future careers that should attract the attention of the comparative historian. It is of obvious significance, for instance, that both Richelieu and Olivares possessed the works of Justus

Lipsius in their libraries and were deeply influenced by his neo-Stoic philosophy, with its detached and ironical perception of human motivations, its emphasis on the importance of discipline and order, and its insistence on prudence as the essential requirement for the statesman.[20] But other coincidences may lead to a dead end – for example, the fact that the two men died at roughly the same age, Richelieu at fifty-seven and Olivares at fifty-eight. The discovery of similarities, such as age at death, or even the hypochondria in which both statesmen indulged, may not, therefore, necessarily be fruitful, although chance resemblances can always be useful for sharpening a vignette or fleshing out a double portrait.

Yet if chance can lead to similarity, so too can imitation. There were many similarities in the reformist policies adopted by Richelieu and Olivares in the early years of their tenure of power. Many of these derived from the context in which the two men were operating – a context in which it appeared necessary to reassert royal authority and mobilize the resources of the state more effectively for war. Yet as rivals for dominance over the Europe of their day, each kept a close watch on what the other was doing, and it is not surprising to find that the Spanish Articles for Reformation of 1623 were published in the *Mercure français* of the same year, and were an obvious source of inspiration for reform proposals put forward by Richelieu shortly afterwards.[21]

This suggests that, while comparative historians need to keep their eyes open for similarities of situation and explain how these might be conducive to similarities of response in their units of comparison, it is important not to rule out the possibility of direct borrowing as a plausible explanation for more or less identical behaviour. Such borrowing may be between contemporaneous societies, but it may also be between the present and the past. Richelieu and Olivares, as rival statesmen, may have been watching each other like two cats, but both sought and found inspiration in the discipline and order exemplified by the Roman examples that Justus Lipsius had taught them to admire. Comparison, if it is to be comprehensive, requires a constant making of connections.

Interconnectedness and the making of connections have in recent years attracted growing attention from social scientists and historians, and stimulated the development of what has come to be called *histoire croisée*, rather unhappily translated as 'entangled histories'.[22] The proponents of *histoire croisée* see it as countering one of the objections that has been raised to comparative history – that the comparative approach assumes a point of view external to the objects that are compared. *Histoire croisée*, by contrast, concentrates on the processes of transfer, between societies, nations or civilizations, and its consequences. This, it is claimed, allows for a multidimensional approach which acknowledges plurality. While this is clearly desirable in so far as it can be achieved, *histoire croisée* may prove to be little more than a new name for an old technique. Historians have always been interested in cultural transfers, and good comparative historians will surely take into account the impact of mutual interaction and of the borrowing and imitation of ideas, institutions and cultural practices on the character and development of their units of comparison. To compare and connect are, and should be treated as, two sides of a single coin.

Writing in 1980 the distinguished American historian George Fredrickson, who went on to publish a fruitful comparison of white supremacy in the United States and South Africa, complained that 'comparative history does not really exist yet as an established field within history or even as a well-defined method of studying history'.[23] Whether it ever can be, or should be, a 'well-defined method', seems to me, however, to be open to question. There are types of comparison and degrees of comparison, all of which have their own possibilities and limitations, and comparative history may be better described as an art than as a method. The German historian Jürgen Kocka, for instance, has advocated what he calls 'asymmetrical comparison', by which he means 'a form of comparison that is centrally interested in describing, explaining and interpreting *one* case, usually one's own case, by contrasting it with others, while the other case or cases are not brought in for their own sake, and are usually not fully researched but only sketched as a kind of background'.[24] This is obviously a more manageable form of comparative history than one which requires the kind of genuinely symmetrical comparison that is so difficult to achieve, either because of the inadequacies of evidence for one unit of comparison or the other, or because of the inability of the historian to achieve an equal mastery of the sources for both. It seems to me, however, to be no less valid a comparative approach than one that looks to a more sustained comparison between the different units. Here, as ever, the exact degree of comparison depends on the kind of questions to be addressed.

It so happens that my own interests pushed me in the direction of the sustained type of comparison. To some extent this had already happened in my attempt to compare Richelieu and Olivares, which may originally have been inspired by my hopes of securing a better understanding of the career and policies of the Count-Duke, but which led me into a more general consideration of the problems of seventeenth-century statesmanship. It was, however, after completing my various studies of Olivares and his Spain that my thoughts turned to the possibility of engaging in a sustained piece of comparative history on a large scale, this time of the societies created by Britain and Spain in the Americas.

Seventeen years spent in a North American environment, and especially the environment of Princeton – still within hailing distance of colonial America, thanks to its university, its battlefield, and its Quaker meeting-house – naturally awakened my interest in the kind of civilization established by my compatriots on that side of the ocean. In contemplating these colonial survivals my thoughts were never far away from the cities and churches that I had seen on my travels in Mexico and Spanish South America. From relatively early years in my study of Spain I had been attracted to the history of Spanish overseas expansion, and had developed a particular interest in Hernán Cortés and the conquest of Mexico, a subject on which I gave a lecture course in Cambridge. It was therefore natural that I should begin to make comparisons in my own mind between the forms of colonization adopted by the Spaniards and the English in America, and between the kinds of societies they established, and the methods by which they governed them.

As I began to think more seriously about these two colonial worlds, and started dipping into the immense literature on the history of British North America, I came to realize that a sustained comparison offered opportunities that might help to shed light on the development not only of the two colonial societies but of the imperial systems of which they formed a part. There was high-quality literature on both British and Spanish colonial America, but I could not fail to be struck by the degree to which the two literatures were unrelated to each other. Each world seemed to exist in a self-contained compartment, with little or no reference to what was happening simultaneously in the other, although the fact that the two touched hands at certain points had led to the development in the United States of a subfield of history of the Spanish borderlands, which, however, remained relatively isolated from the mainstream of North American history. This had taken a course of its own, characterized by a profound belief in the exceptional character of the United States and its manifest destiny. The societies developed by the Spaniards in their American possessions offered at best a useful counterpoint to the history of the United States by illustrating in dramatic form what was assumed to be the innate superiority of Anglo-American to Iberian civilization.

In undertaking a comparison between British and Spanish America I was far from sailing in uncharted waters. Already in

the eighteenth century the comparison was being made, especially by the English and the inhabitants of their colonies, and it
was usually made in order to demonstrate the superiority of an
English 'empire of commerce' to a Spanish 'empire of conquest'.
As the United States forged ahead in the nineteenth century
while the new republics that emerged from the wreckage of
Spain's American empire appeared to be incapable of achieving
political stability and economic success, the assertions of North
American superiority became more strident and the criticisms of
Latin American societies more acute. During the twentieth
century the reasons for the 'failure of Latin America' as set against
the story of a triumphant United States became a favourite topic
of political and social scientists, economists and historians.

There were, however, exceptions, even in the Anglo-
American world, to the generally negative verdict on Latin
America. One of the most notable of these emerged out of the
comparative study of New World slavery. In 1946 Frank
Tannenbaum, whose seminars at Columbia University I
attended in 1963, published his seminal work *Slave and
Citizen*, in which he examined the legal systems of British and
Spanish America, and argued that slaves in the Iberian world
were treated less harshly by their masters than their counter-
parts in British America.[25] Tannenbaum's book, while not itself
strictly a comparative history, stimulated a valuable and continuing debate involving comparisons of the theory, practice and
cultural context of African slavery in the Americas.[26]

Slavery offered, and still offers, an obvious point of comparison. More unexpected was the foray into American comparative

history of the classical historian Ronald Syme, with a set of lectures comparing the role of Spaniards in imperial Rome and the behaviour of British and Spanish American colonial elites.[27] Syme, by origin a New Zealander, was especially interested in the relationship of provincial or colonial elites to the imperial centre and in their contribution to its life. In this tripartite comparison, Spanish Romans emerged as the clear winners. While Syme's slender volume did little more than touch on the composition, character and behaviour of colonial elites, it identified a subject with significant implications for the long-term stability and survival of the empires he discussed.

Syme's work was essentially a trial balloon that soared into the empyrean and then, unlike Tannenbaum's study of slavery, disappeared from sight. In 1975, however, a social scientist, James Lang, attempted a wide-ranging comparison of British and Spanish colonial America under the title of *Conquest and Commerce*.[28] The title harked back to the eighteenth-century distinction between the two empires, and the effect of the book was to underline the sharpness of the contrast by showing how the beginnings of the empires shaped their differing development and that of the colonial societies they created. In this sense, Lang's book followed the path taken earlier by Louis Hartz, also a social scientist, whose *The Founding of New Societies* depicted European overseas settlements as 'fragments of the larger whole of Europe struck off in the course of the revolution which brought the west into the modern world', and argued that they were programmed from the first by the timing of their origin.[29]

Although Lang's *Conquest and Commerce* was lucid and informative, it seemed to me inadequate as a sustained comparison of the two empires and the colonial societies they originated. In terms of content, it gained coherence from presenting the view from the metropolis, but I felt that it suffered from taking as a given the long-term implications of the conquest/commerce dichotomy that allegedly characterized the initial stages of colonization, while ignoring the impact of changing circumstances. Lang's approach to the task of comparison also left me dissatisfied. In dividing his book into two separate parts, the first dealing with Spanish America and the second with British America, he opted for juxtaposition rather than for sustained comparison, which only came in the form of a brief conclusion.

As I contemplated the problems and the possibilities, I sensed that there was an opportunity for a book that would resemble Lang's in its chronological scope, running as it did from the beginnings of colonization to the coming of independence, but that it needed to be more ambitious than Lang in comparing and contrasting. This was to be as sustained a comparison as I could make it. The dominant contemporary question of the 'success' of the United States as against the alleged 'failure' of Latin America would inevitably hover in the background of any such comparison, but I was anxious to avoid making this the theme of the book, although I had no doubt that some of my readers would approach it with this in mind. Instead, my hope was to set the two colonial worlds firmly in the context of their own time, rather than viewing them retrospectively through the lens of nineteenth- and twentieth-century developments. The obvious wealth and prosperity of late eighteenth-century Mexico, as depicted by Alexander von Humboldt, serves as a salutary reminder that its subsequent eclipse by the British settlements in North America was at the time by no means a foregone conclusion.

It was, I suppose, a historian's view of the history of the two Americas that I wanted to project, with space given to the unexpected, the contingent and the unpredictable. It was only after my retirement from my Oxford chair in 1997 that I was able to settle down to planning and writing the book, eventually published in 2006 as *Empires of the Atlantic World*,[30] but I had used the preceding years to try to get abreast of the massive amount of work that had been published on British American colonial history, while at the same time deepening my knowledge of Spain's empire of the Indies. The ultimate challenge would no doubt be a comparative survey of all the European empires in the Americas – French, Dutch and Portuguese, as well as Spanish and British – but it was hard enough to keep up with the rapidly proliferating literature on two empires without adding three more. It also seemed to me that, if I did so, I would be faced with one of the central dilemmas of comparative history: that the greater the number of the units of comparison, the more diluted the comparison becomes.

To some extent I was motivated by a desire to test the possibilities and the limitations of comparative history itself. Could it, as I hoped, help to break down what I saw as the artificial compartmentalization of the history of British and Iberian

America, and, in doing so, challenge the assumptions of Anglo-American, Spanish and Latin American historians about the uniqueness of their own particular civilizations? At the very least a comparative perspective might help to broaden historical horizons. While it was perfectly possible that the kind of study I had in mind would not actually answer many of the questions traditionally asked about the two colonial worlds, and ran the obvious risk of telling specialist readers what they already knew, I felt that it would have served its turn if it helped to suggest new questions and stimulate new thinking. A close comparative study, as distinct from a study of two imperial enterprises placed in juxtaposition, ought, for instance, to raise fundamental questions about the nature of European overseas expansion and settlement in the sixteenth and seventeenth centuries. How far, for example, were English and Castilian transatlantic enterprises driven by the same imperatives, and to what extent did the colonizers face similar problems and resort to similar methods to solve them? What were the similarities and what the differences between the British and Spanish transatlantic settlements, and how are they to be explained? Or, moving into the eighteenth century, how far were the movements for independence generated by the same forces in British and Spanish America, and how was it that Spain managed to hold on to its American empire half a century longer than a Britain that was unable to retain control of thirteen mainland colonies?

The problems that faced me in the writing may serve to illustrate the kind of difficulties that confront any aspiring comparative historian. As a historian I wanted to convey a sense of movement and change through time, rather than base my comparison on a photographic view of two societies caught at a given moment by the click of a camera. This required a narrative approach, in so far as I was attempting to tell two separate but connected stories, interweaving them but comparing and contrasting as I went along. At the same time, while sceptical about the possibilities of producing any grand theory, I was anxious to allow space for analysis, but in such a way as not to impede the flow of the narrative. This is a challenge that faces all narrative historians, but it is inevitably complicated when the stories to be told are not one but two or more.

Beyond the problem of presentation, which, like all historical writing that seeks to combine narrative and analysis, provides a continuing test of literary skills, I became increasingly aware of the need to bear constantly in mind a number of variables that would shape, and might well distort, the comparisons that I wanted to make. All comparative historians working on a broad canvas are likely to come across such variables in one form or another. The first of the variables I encountered, and one that proved to be particularly acute in a comparison of two empires over three centuries, was that of chronological disparity. England embarked on the acquisition and colonization of American territory more than a century after Castile. This, moreover, was a century of transformative change in Europe, as a result of the Protestant Reformation, the intensification of national rivalries, and, not least, the fact that by the end of the century Spain's acquisition of a silver-rich American empire had made it the dominant European power. The approach of the English to overseas settlement could not fail to reflect these influences. Their religion, their culture, their politics, had all been profoundly affected by the changes. Moreover, they had the Spanish example before them as they set out on their colonial enterprise. Where they consciously followed it, or even where equally consciously they refused to do so, their efforts exemplified the importance for the comparative historian of incorporating *histoire croisée* into the comparison.

The time-lag of a century inevitably changes the nature of a comparison that would have been more straightforward if Spain and England had founded their colonies at roughly the same moment. Yet it could be argued that differences of timing were ultimately of less significance to the character of the colonizing process than environmental differences. Geography and climate impose their own imperatives. While the Caribbean islands provide a relatively homogeneous environment for a close historical comparison of a kind that is yet to be attempted, the American mainland reached by the Europeans was characterized by enormous climatic and ecological variations. To settle in the high Andes was a very different proposition from settling in the coastal regions of North America. Nor was the difference purely climatic and ecological. The Europeans intruded on lands that were already populated, more or less heavily, by an enormous variety of peoples. The nature of these peoples and the density of their settlement patterns were bound to have a decisive impact on the behaviour of European conquerors and colonists as they sought to impose their own presence. So, too, were the wide variations in the natural and mineral resources to be found in the Americas, some coveted by Europeans and some not. What part did the existence of these resources play in determining the different trajectories of their respective empires?

Alongside the variables created by differences of timing and environment are those that arise from the differing histories, traditions, laws, culture and values of the colonizing countries – what David Hume called their 'national character'. Hume pointed to the differences between the English, French and Dutch colonies, even in a tropical environment, as evidence of the greater influence exerted over the colonists by nurture than by nature.[31] Whatever the weight to be assigned by cultural inheritances, they clearly have to be factored into the comparative equation. Culture, however, is not a static phenomenon, and national character is not set in stone. Once again the changes wrought by time have to be borne in mind.

Finally, any historical comparison has to take into account the human variables – the role, for instance, of outstanding individuals, a George Washington or a Simón Bolívar, in shaping the course of events. In a comparison of imperial systems much depends on the willingness and the effectiveness of individual agents of imperial government in carrying out its orders, just as it also depends on the responses of the governed, which similarly will depend on individual action as well as on collective attitudes.

With variables on such a scale, all comparisons are bound to be flawed. Reviewers of *Empires of the Atlantic World* rightly identified some of the topics that the book underplayed or ignored. Some felt that it concentrated excessively on the settler communities to the detriment of the indigenous peoples of the Americas and of African slaves. Others thought that my concentration on the heartlands of empire – the British mainland colonies on the one hand and Mexico and Peru on the other – at the expense of the British West Indies and the more peripheral regions of Spain's empire in America gave a distorted picture which tended to vitiate my comparisons. Against this, one reviewer argued that in a book which identifies the commonalities in imperial assumptions, a comparison between Peru and New England highlights the differences in colonial structures more effectively than a comparison between Cuba and Jamaica.[32] Since I was concerned with identifying differences as much as similarities, and then seeking to explain them, this was certainly my hope.

Selectivity in a comparative enterprise of this kind is inevitable, and no one is likely to be more conscious than the author of the problems of inclusion and omission that it entails. My purpose was not, as some would have liked, to advance a bold new thesis about the development of the British and Spanish empires in America, but rather to make a set of comparisons that might help to focus attention on such major historical problems as the relative weight to be given to culture and environment in particular situations. Here I was struck by the way in which the American environment had the effect in the settler communities of reinforcing certain characteristics found in the home society at the expense of others. The discovery, for example, of large settled populations and rich mineral resources in Mexico and Peru naturally reinforced among the colonists the tendency that can be observed in medieval Castilian society to equate wealth with lordship and plunder, whereas their absence in British North America encouraged the settlers to have recourse to those values and practices in their home society that would enable them to survive in their new and apparently unpromising environment. Above all, however, I was anxious to offer what I hoped would be new and unexpected insights into the structure, workings and character of one empire by means of a close comparison with the other. It remains to be seen whether the book has any impact on the way in which the history of these two empires has conventionally been written.

Ultimately all historical exposition and analysis are essentially a search for the greatest possible degree of plausibility in the exploration and interpretation of the past. While, as Marc Bloch said, 'in science, there is no talisman', the comparative method that he so forcefully advocated is one among the many useful devices at the disposal of the historian in the search for that elusive goal. No more than any other form of history does it have all the answers, but, after experiencing some of its excitements and grappling with its challenges, I remain persuaded that Bloch's eloquent plea for the wider practice of comparative history deserves a more generous response than it has hitherto received.

CHAPTER SEVEN

The wider picture

I<small>N</small> a review of the publications of Christopher Hill on the history of seventeenth-century England, the American historian J. H. Hexter famously divided historians into 'lumpers' and 'splitters'. 'Historians who are splitters', he tells us, 'like to point out divergences, to perceive differences, to draw distinctions. They shrink away from systems of history and from general rules, and carry around in their heads lists of exceptions to almost any rule they are likely to encounter. They do not mind untidiness and accident in the past; they rather like them.' 'Lumpers', on the other hand, would prefer to see untidiness and accident vanish. Instead of noting differences, they 'note likenesses; instead of separateness, connection. The lumping historian wants to put the past into boxes, all of it, and not too many boxes at that, and then to tie all the boxes together into one nice shapely bundle.'[1]

A comparable distinction was later drawn by the French historian Emmanuel Le Roy Ladurie, who divided historians into parachutists and truffle hunters.[2] As he subsequently confirmed for me, in writing of parachutists he did not have in mind, as is generally assumed, those who take a bird's-eye perspective, but French soldiers who scoured large areas of territory in the war in Algeria around 1960. Some historians, like these parachutists, range widely over the terrain, while others, like truffle hunters, dig down to unearth a buried treasure.[3]

Whatever the precise shade of meaning in their respective distinctions, both Hexter and Ladurie were differentiating between two kinds of historian, and two different approaches to the historical enterprise, one of which is intensive and narrowly focused, while the other is broad-gauged and wide-ranging. To some extent, the difference is a reflection of a tension between the generalizing and the particular within the writing of history as it has developed in the western world. To some extent, too, it reflects temperamental differences among historians, some of whom are by nature pointillistes, instinctively drawn to the making of neat and precise marks on the canvas, while others prefer the broad brushstroke. In practice, the division is not necessarily as clear-cut as the categorization of historians into splitters and lumpers, or truffle hunters and parachutists, would suggest. Many historians are perfectly capable of adopting both approaches, and move with ease in either direction in response to the nature of the evidence and of the problem to be solved. Ideally, the two approaches should not be incompatible, and at their best they can yield a synthesis in which the particular and the general blend. Yet the intense professionalization of the subject, the enormous increase in the number of historians, and the proliferation of academic theses have all had the effect, during much of my working lifetime, of encouraging a delimitation of the past into small areas of territory that researchers can plausibly claim as their own. The price of this territorial mastery is all too often a narrowing of focus, and ultimately a loss of historical nerve.

For some years now, however, a reaction has been under way, and it appears to be gathering momentum. There are many reasons for this. The narrowing of focus has itself generated a reaction in the opposite direction – a reaction that has been fed by a growing public demand for accessible accounts of the past which highly specialized historians, accustomed to talking largely among themselves, have seemed incapable of providing. This has led to the rise of a new breed of historians who have used television and radio to explain and interpret the past to large audiences, although with varying degrees of success in so far as the maintenance of scholarly standards is concerned. It is not easy to simplify the past while simultaneously fostering an awareness of its complexity.

Perhaps more important in expanding the range of history and moving it in new directions has been a growing disenchantment with traditional categories and an impatience with traditional boundaries. Multitudes had been excluded from the top-down approach that characterized so much nineteenth- and twentieth-century writing about the past: the socially and politically marginalized, the exploited and the downtrodden, and all those who stood on the wrong side of histories written from the vantage-point of the victors. Where, too, were women – half the human race? Even if the record was hardly as bleak as the mounting tide of criticism might suggest, there was a justified sense that all too many had not been given their historical due.

Standard historical categories were meanwhile being subjected to close scrutiny as a result of the sweeping changes in the character of the world in which historians found themselves living. For all the publicity nowadays given to 'globalization', the notion of a single world is hardly a new one. The eyes of sixteenth-century Europeans were opened by the voyages of exploration, the results of which they could follow on their maps and globes. 'All men', wrote Jean Bodin, 'surprisingly work together in a world state, as if in one and the same city-state.'[4] His observation may have been premature, but both physically and conceptually it reflected the fact that the process of globalization had begun. By the late twentieth century, the speed with which knowledge could be transmitted and ideas and images diffused made that single city-state a reality in ways of which Bodin could never have conceived.

One of the effects of the new surge of globalization was to make much writing about the past look suddenly parochial. The history of individual nation states and even of empires began to look excessively constricted in a world struggling to come to terms with the consequences of climate change and the pace of globalization. As the environmental historian Alfred Crosby memorably noted, the empire of the dandelion is the one empire on which the sun never sets.[5] The challenge that presented itself to many historians was to transcend the limited and the parochial in response to a world undergoing a process of transformation that was ruthlessly sweeping the old barriers aside. Historical writing about states and empires felt the impact of this transformation, although in reality there were many precedents for the great upsurge of transnational and trans-imperial history at the turn of the twentieth and twenty-first centuries. Braudel's *Méditerranée*, after all, was a work that soared blithely over national boundaries in its attempt to evoke the characteristics of a civilization defined by an inner sea. Politics and geo-politics alike encouraged historians to widen their frame of reference, or helped to create new mind-sets that would enable them to do so.

A prime example of this process has been the emergence of an 'Atlantic history' that has sought to break free of national and imperial boundaries. Its sources have been traced back to the Second World War and the era of the Atlantic community, although there are earlier precedents.[6] The creation of the North Atlantic Treaty Organization and the perceived importance of an Atlantic Alliance that would bind together the western world during the period of the Cold War undoubtedly generated governmental and private initiatives that encouraged Atlanticist thinking, but it is not easy to determine the degree to which these influenced historical inquiry. As far as I am aware, the Wiles Lectures which I delivered at the Queen's University, Belfast, in 1969, and which were published the following year under the title *The Old World and the New, 1492–1650*,[7] had very little to do with the political context, and much more to do with my own personal experience and the historical literature that I had been absorbing in the preceding years.

The brief of these lectures was to encourage the discussion of broad issues relating to the general history of civilization. This pointed to the need for a subject that transcended purely national history, and the theme that suggested itself arose directly out of what I had recently been doing and thinking. In 1963–4 I was granted a year's sabbatical leave by Cambridge University. I had long felt the need to extend my knowledge and understanding of the history of early modern Spain by looking at the conquest and government of its empire in America, and my sabbatical would allow me not only to make contact with historians of Latin America but also to see for myself some of the lands colonized by Spain. It should, however, be noted that a growing national preoccupation with the decline of British influence in Latin America, and the appointment of a national committee, the Parry Committee, to encourage the study of Latin America in British university departments, made this a particularly propitious moment for an extension of my interests into Iberian American history. Historians are never quite as independent of contemporary preoccupations as they would like to believe.

Some seven months of travel around Latin America, beginning in Mexico and ending in Venezuela, gave me a feeling for a world that I had hitherto known only from books. The first and perhaps most lasting impression was that of almost infinite space. The streets of colonial cities, laid out in the Spanish

manner on a grid-iron pattern, led outwards to empty landscapes that stretched far into the distance. The other abiding
impression was that of the extraordinary variety – ecological,
ethnic, cultural – of this vast and infinitely rich New World on
which the Spaniards were the first Europeans to set eyes, and
which they sought to mould in their image. In the valley of
Mexico, in Yucatán and the high Andes, the relics of the civilizations they had overwhelmed were everywhere to be seen.
High up in the cold, thin air of modern-day Bolivia the colonial
city of Potosí, clustering around the foot of its ochre-coloured
mountain, stands as a lasting reminder of that combination of
Spanish enterprise and Indian suffering which launched the
first wave of globalization on a flood-tide of silver.

As I contemplated this New World that I had now discovered for myself, and then reflected on it after my return, I
wanted to see it through the eyes of sixteenth-century
Spaniards. This led me to explore the works of the early
chroniclers with a view to discovering how they saw and interpreted the sights that unfolded before them and struggled to
explain the origins and characteristics of the strange peoples
with whom they came into contact. The immensely rich body
of writings they produced made me realize the possibilities
these offered for examining the reaction of Europeans to their
encounter with the non-European peoples of the world. I was
encouraged in this by my reading of the work of Antonello
Gerbi (1904–76), an Italian banker whose professional
concerns did not prevent him from producing some impressive
studies of European responses to America, including most

notably *The Dispute of the New World,* a fascinating account of the great debate, conducted on both sides of the Atlantic, over the natural history of the Americas and the characteristics of their peoples.[8]

In thinking about these sixteenth-century sources with the invitation to give the Wiles Lectures in mind, it struck me that while a great deal had been written about the impact of Spain on America, much less had been written about the impact of the discovery of America on Spain. The great exception was in the field of economic history, where Earl J. Hamilton had studied the inflationary impact on Spanish prices of the silver consignments arriving in Seville each year from the Mexican mines and Potosí. More recently Pierre and Huguette Chaunu had launched a flotilla of volumes, heavily freighted with statistics, with the intention of charting the course of Spain's Atlantic economy over a period of a century and a half.[9] But the consequences of Spanish exploitation of the resources of the New World extended far beyond the Iberian peninsula itself. All Spain's activities in America had their European implications, and the reports of Spanish observers and actors percolated through the continent. Those reports shaped Europe's collective images of the New World and its inhabitants, and influenced the attitudes and behaviour of other European nationalities when they in turn came face to face with the indigenous peoples of America.

These considerations led me to frame the Wiles Lectures in terms of a European rather than an exclusively Spanish response to the conquest and colonization of America, although the Spaniards, as was to be expected, were the principal agents and actors in my telling of the story. My object in *The Old World and the New* was to examine, in the succinct form imposed by a lecture series, what seemed to me to be the principal intellectual, economic and geo-political consequences for Europe of the intrusion of Europeans into an American world of whose existence they had previously been unaware. The last chapter of the book was entitled 'The Atlantic World'. Like Molière's *bourgeois gentilhomme* who discovered that for forty years he had been speaking prose without knowing it, I was later to find that in the late 1960s I had been writing Atlantic history without being conscious of the fact.

'We are all Atlanticists now', wrote one of its most effective spokesmen in an influential essay first published in 2002.[10] These perhaps over-confident words were written at a time when Atlantic history seemed to be sweeping all before it. The attractions of an Atlanticist approach were obvious. There was an undoubted weariness with traditional imperial and colonial history, and a feeling that many subjects had been run into the ground. Yet, as happens so often, contemporary concerns also intervened to shape historians' perceptions of the past. In an age increasingly dominated by networking and the making of connections it was natural to search for past networks and connections that had escaped the notice of earlier historians locked into their national boxes. The Atlantic Ocean, joining and separating three continents, appeared the perfect arena for the writing of such interconnected histories. The outcome was a lively and innovative historiography that, by concentrating on human diasporas, and on the movement of people, commodities, ideas and cultural practices around and across the Atlantic, revealed often unsuspected connections, shaping new ethnic groupings and communities, and constantly subverting the frontier lines drawn on European maps.

Inevitably, however, at the same time as the possibilities of Atlantic history were becoming apparent, so too were some of its limitations. How far, for instance, is it historically legitimate to speak of an 'Atlantic world'? In one of the few successful attempts to make the ocean itself, rather than the regions that bordered it, the centre of the story, Ian Steele reminds us that, for most of the eighteenth century, the 'Atlantic' to British eyes was no more than the North Atlantic. Anything further south was the 'Ethiopean Sea'.[11] During the sixteenth, seventeenth and eighteenth centuries different European states developed different transatlantic routes, whose trajectories were determined by the regions of the American hemisphere in which they were primarily interested, and by the winds and currents that could carry them there. As these routes became systematized, starting with the route followed by Columbus between Andalusia and the Indies, we can begin to speak of a number of Atlantics – Spanish, Portuguese, English, Dutch and French. The historian who hopes to span these several Atlantics, however, requires impressive linguistic skills and a wide range of reading. In the circumstances, it is not surprising that, in spite of its ambitions, much of the Atlantic history so far written has tended to remain within the parameters of individual national Atlantics.

From the mid-seventeenth century onwards, as these different Atlantics in turn became interconnected through trade and contraband, and west Africa came to be fully incorporated into the international network through the development of the slave trade, it becomes possible to trace the elaboration of a genuinely pan-Atlantic system, connecting at a growing number of points the many communities living along the European, American and African shores of the ocean. But it seems hard to accept the existence of anything like an integrated Atlantic before the later nineteenth century. Even then, it could be argued that, with Africa playing a diminished part in migratory movements following the abolition of the slave trade, the Atlantic community around 1900 was overwhelmingly a European-Atlantic community, which only began to recover something of its African dimension with the rise of black consciousness in the later twentieth century.[12]

The hypothesis of a single Atlantic civilization embracing both sides of the ocean therefore seems an even more dubious proposition than that of a Mediterranean civilization, which, although religiously divided between Christians and Muslims, at least possessed many common features as a result of bordering the shores of an enclosed sea. Yet if the Atlantic is no Mediterranean and thus lacked some of the possibilities for the sharing of characteristics that comes from relative proximity within an enclosed space, this does not necessarily preclude the notion of the Atlantic world as a viable unit of study, as long as we think of it as a world whose degree of integration has fluctuated and will continue to fluctuate over time, and in response to varying influences and needs.

The fact, too, that the Atlantic is not an enclosed but an open space means that its geographical like its chronological limits escape easy definition. Spain's viceroyalty of Peru, for instance, with its long Pacific coastline, hardly looks like a candidate for inclusion in the Atlantic world. Yet the silver extracted from the silver mountain of Potosí and shipped from the Pacific port of Callao to the isthmus of Panama, and from there to Seville, was fundamental to the operations of Spain's Atlantic economy.[13] As a result, the viceroyalty from its early years was well and truly integrated into the Spanish Atlantic system, but in spite of this it can hardly be described, as colonial New England can reasonably be described, as an Atlantic society. The same is true, and perhaps to an even greater degree, of the Mexican viceroyalty of New Spain. The conquest of the Philippines in the reign of Philip II and their subsequent incorporation into the Mexican viceroyalty opened up trans-Pacific trading links that brought painted screens and large quantities of Chinese porcelains and silks to Mexico and Peru. Not surprisingly, by 1600 the creole elite of New Spain were beginning to think of Mexico as the centre of the world, facing not only across the Atlantic to Europe but also across the Pacific to the fabled lands of Asia.

If neither Mexico nor Peru can be seen as an exclusively Atlantic society, in spite of the European origins and affiliations of their settlers, comparable problems arise in relation to the indigenous peoples of the Americas. It is undeniable that a ripple effect, travelling from the Atlantic to the Pacific coast, brought profound changes to the Indian nations of the interior as it passed their way. But it would be hard to classify most of these peoples as citizens, however involuntary, of a developing Atlantic world. If the majority of them do not fall within the ambit of Atlantic history they should be allowed to retain their historiographical independence, just as they long managed to retain their physical and spiritual independence on the North American plains. The same consideration would surely apply to the peoples of sub-Saharan Africa, who, at least before the eighteenth and nineteenth centuries, were as likely to be carried into slavery across the Sahara as to be transported westwards across the Atlantic.

None of this means in itself that Atlantic history is not viable, but it does suggest that Atlantic historians would be unwise to claim hegemonic rights. There were worlds beyond the Atlantic, and growing numbers of European merchants, soldiers, sailors, officials and clerics travelled into and out of these worlds, often crossing and recrossing the Atlantic, but also moving into Asia and Africa, as they went about their business. Along with emigrants, seeking better opportunities on the far side of the Atlantic, there were also thousands upon thousands who travelled involuntarily, whether as captives, convicts or slaves. Much of this movement took place within the framework of Europe's expanding empires, and the travels of individual men and women caught up in the web of empire have recently become the subject of much historical interest, incidentally renovating the biographical approach by concentrating on the lives of forgotten or relatively unimportant figures, made interesting by the nature and extent of their travels and their intercontinental connections.[14]

Movement and connection lie at the heart of Atlantic history as currently practised, and the bias is understandable, given the fluidity and interconnectedness of life in today's world. But those who study earlier ages through this contemporary lens run the risk of forgetting what the Australian historian Geoffrey Blainey memorably called 'the tyranny of distance'.[15] If there was what now seems an unexpected amount of movement around and across the Atlantic in earlier centuries, there were also numerous interruptions to the flow of people and goods. Maritime lifelines were fragile, and made precarious by winds and waves, and by piracy and war. Activity was punctuated by long periods of silence, and of waiting for ships and supplies that never arrived. Isolation could all too easily turn out to be the fate of many of those thousands of 'Europeans on the move',[16] as the English settlers left behind on Roanoke Island in the 1580s found to their cost. Fluidity may have been a characteristic of the Atlantic world for much of its history since the end of the fifteenth century, but so also, and in perhaps greater measure, was stasis, which lacks the drama of movement.

The new Atlantic history has performed a valuable service in demonstrating the porous nature of European empires, and the ease with which people, goods and ideas moved across imperial borderlines. But, at the same time, movement was in some degree constrained and held in check by the institutions of empire, by law and bureaucracy and by the exercise of brute force. If empire created channels for movement, it also had it in its power to create blockages, and the activities of empire, as both obstacle and enabler, give imperial history its continuing relevance at a time when the study of connections, as exemplified by Atlantic history, has become a dominant interest.

The collapse and disappearance of Europe's overseas empires during the course of the twentieth century, the disintegration of the Soviet empire and the faltering of American power have combined to give imperial history a new lease of life, as formal empires have ceased to be a lived experience and are transformed into historical phenomena. Imperial history lived for some time under a shadow during the middle decades of the twentieth century, in part because of the general discrediting of empire in the period after the Second World War, and in part because of its unfashionable institutional bias. Since then, however, fresh historical approaches have made clear its continuing potential. Historians and anthropologists have struggled with some success over the past few decades to recover 'the vision of the vanquished' and to give back their past to 'the people without history'.[17] A great process of rethinking the character of the relationships between colonists and colonized has revealed something of their extraordinary complexity by restoring a degree of agency to the 'victims', and exposing the existence of a 'middle ground' on which 'diverse peoples adjust their differences through what amounts to a process of creative, and often expedient, misunderstandings'.[18] At the same time, the new emphasis placed by later twentieth-century historians on social and cultural history and the history of representation has helped to breathe new life into the history of imperial institutions and the study of imperial ideologies.

Yet it has become increasingly clear that, even as imperial history has rejuvenated itself, 'empire' suffers, as an organizing concept, from the same kind of deficiencies as 'nation' and 'state'. Like Atlantic history, the history of empires transcends standard geographical boundaries and cries out to be set in a global context. The rise of 'world history', as it has developed since the 1980s, has been, at least in part, a response to the perceived inadequacies of traditional historical categories. Once again the study of networks, connections and interacting systems has become a key to unlocking the past.

A distinction deserves to be drawn, however, between world history which seeks to place national or imperial history in a global context, and world history seen as a history of the process, or progress, of globalization. Both are currently being illuminated by the tracing of connections and the drawing of comparisons, and sometimes simply by imaginative juxtaposition – for instance, by deploying a series of vignettes of local sights and scenes around the globe to evoke a picture of how the world looked and behaved at a given moment in the past.[19] This approach has all the strengths and weaknesses of the current trend for connective history as exemplified by Atlantic history. Sometimes the connections provide new and unexpected insights into how people and civilizations came into contact with each other, and how this affected their outlook and behaviour. At other times, the connections are no more than those in the mind of the historian, attempting to provide a conceptual framework for the exploration of a theme designed to illuminate developments on a global scale. In this macrohistorical approach the particular is liable to lose out to the general. It is not easy to see how a multitude of smaller histories can convincingly be made commensurable with a genuinely global history that spans the world from China to Peru.

Much of the current move into world history, however, has taken the form of describing and analysing the process of globalization. While this is a history that needs to be written, it all too easily becomes a story that begins with 'Europe' and ends with 'modernity', a concept that itself is defined in western or European terms. While it was Europeans who, through their voyages and travels, did more than the peoples of any other continent to bring the world together, there were wide variations in the impact of their presence. If conquest and colonization enabled them to shape new civilizations in the Americas, the old civilizations of Asia and Africa proved for long resistant, or relatively impervious, to their ways of thought and action. From the late eighteenth century to the early twentieth its military and technological superiority gave the west its edge, and in that sense globalization can be seen as a reflection of the west's attempts to export or impose its own products, culture and values. Yet the process of transmission was erratic, the degree of acceptance uneven, and the consequences would often prove counter-productive.

The equation of those western products and values with 'modernity' implies a division of the world into societies that either cling to the past or embrace the future. It also reflects a Eurocentric view of global history which underestimates the contribution of non-western societies to the making of the contemporary world. That Eurocentric approach has understandably come to be challenged by those who observe the economic vibrancy of many parts of Asia, the Middle East and Africa in the period before 1800, and question the degree to which an industrializing Europe held all the cards.[20] The resulting debate over what has come to be known as 'the great divergence'[21] – the economic divide between an advanced west and the rest of the world – has led to important revisionist discussions not only of the economies of China and India in the pre-industrial era, but also of standard interpretations of the Industrial Revolution of the late eighteenth and early nineteenth centuries in northwestern Europe. If that revolution is recast to incorporate the concept of an 'industrious revolution'[22] during the seventeenth and eighteenth centuries – a 'revolution' that was by no means confined to western societies – the European experience loses something of its novelty and uniqueness, and the 'great divergence', coinciding with two centuries of western triumphalism and imperial hegemony, appears in the context of world history as a transient although massively transformative phenomenon that is now approaching its end.

Recent work on industrialization has made it clear that what has traditionally been known as the Industrial Revolution can only be fully understood if it is placed in a global context and treated on a global scale. This requires, as with all history, the making of connections – the connections, for example, between the establishment of slave-based plantation economies in the Caribbean, the growth of consumer societies in eighteenth-century Europe, and the development of the textile industry in the Indian subcontinent – and also the drawing of comparisons. A globalizing world needs authentically global history, and this in turn requires a shedding of western prejudices and preconceptions.[23] It also requires an avoidance of the kind of teleological approach that sees all roads leading to 'modernity'.

Modernity is not singular but plural, as S. N. Eisenstadt recognized when he wrote of 'multiple modernities'; and 'modernity' should not be automatically equated with westernization.[24] Societies take their own paths, and bend to the winds of their own traditions, even when – as increasingly happens in a world connected by the almost instantaneous transmission of information – they are affected and influenced by global fashions, trends and movements. To make sense of the contemporary world is a legitimate and desirable part of the historical enterprise, but it is not the whole part, and it requires a willingness and an ability to see that world from a variety of standpoints and with an awareness of the alternatives – benign or pernicious, depending on the perspective adopted – to the dominant paradigm. If, for instance, that paradigm is defined in terms of the progressive advance of science, rationalism and secularization, the search for 'modernity' is liable to lead up a blind alley. As global developments in the late twentieth and early twenty-first centuries have made abundantly plain, the stronger the emphasis on secularization, the greater are the chances of religious revival. The advance of science finds its antithesis in the advance of fundamentalism, and the supranationalism of a world of multinational corporations and organizations finds itself challenged by the upsurge of the 'irrational' forces of old-style nationalism. The past has an uncanny way of coming back to upset the present, and when history is thrown out of the window with a pitchfork, it can be counted upon to return.

If the study of the past has any value, that value lies in its ability to reveal the complexities of human experience, and to counsel against ruling out as of no significance any of the paths that were only partially followed, or not followed at all. At some turn in the road, they may once again come unexpectedly into view. The recognition that the present is full of surprises requires a similar recognition that the past was equally so in the eyes of those who lived it. The challenge that faces the historian is to see and experience that past through their eyes, while knowing, yet trying not to know, what happened afterwards. It is to make the motives for their actions comprehensible to those who do not share their values, attitudes and outlook, and who live in a very different environment. It is to enter imaginatively into the past while still maintaining one foot in the present, and always to be alert to new ways of approaching it.

In surveying the changes in approaches to the past over the course of my lifetime I have concentrated on those most closely related to my own particular interests. As a consequence I have inevitably paid little or no attention to changes of method and fashion in areas or periods of history which have not directly impinged on my own, and which may well be regarded as of greater importance and interest than those that happen to have attracted me. History has become a house with many mansions, and each has been undergoing sometimes exciting expansion and renovation, as well as being threatened by the demolition squads. The history of literature and the history of religion, to take two obvious examples, have developed their own subdisciplines and have expanded to embrace new territory as the number of their practitioners has grown and fresh avenues of approach have been explored.

Historical writing draws its inspiration from curiosity, and as long as curiosity remains, so also do the opportunities. These opportunities have been vastly expanded by the increase in the amount of easily accessible information generated by the digitizing of books and archives. Yet digitization also has its dangers, foreshadowed in the words of the chorus in T. S. Eliot's *The Rock*:

Where is the wisdom we have lost in knowledge?
Where is the knowledge we have lost in information?[25]

Good history will continue to depend, as it has always depended, on something more than the amassing of information and the deployment of knowledge. Every historian's approach to the past is shaped by personal temperament and experience, but no historian is an island unto himself or herself, and wisdom is acquired, at least in part, from reading and reflecting on the work of past and present historians, and consciously participating in a collective enterprise that spans the generations and is committed to achieving a better appreciation both of the world that is gone and of the world as we know it today.

Like so many historians I have felt the sense of personal enrichment that comes from engaging with other participants in this common enterprise. Like them I owe a deep debt to predecessors whose works have inspired and informed my own; to the archivists who have struggled, often in the most unfavourable circumstances, to conserve and classify the documents in their care; and to colleagues, students and readers whose queries, criticisms and comments have stimulated me to formulate or revise my views and to think about old questions in new ways. Above all I am grateful to a long line of graduate students and assistants who have done so much to keep their former mentor up to the mark and whose achievements have been a source of continuing pride.

Much remains to be done. Even within the area of my own special interests, there is still a great deal to be learned about some of the themes touched upon in the pages of this book, like the capacity for survival of Spain's global empire and the particular ways in which politics, culture and society interacted in the Hispanic and early modern European worlds. Great possibilities await the historian brave enough, as I never was, to face the difficulties of mastering Ottoman Turkish and write a modern version of Ranke's *The Ottoman and the Spanish Empires*.[26] More importantly, even in fields that may at first sight appear overcrowded, understanding can always be enhanced by fresh insights and ideas. It is understanding that lies at the heart of the historical enterprise, and this book will have served its purpose if it is read as the testimony of a historian who has tried to understand.

Notes

Preface

1. Rudyard Kipling, *The Complete Verse* (London, 2006), p. 272 ('In the Neolithic Age').

1 Why Spain?

1. For the tradition of British Hispanism, see David Howarth, *The Invention of Spain: Cultural Relations between Britain and Spain, 1770–1870* (Manchester, 2007), and Tom Burns Marañón, *Hispanomanía* (Barcelona, 2000), which continues the story into the twentieth century.
2. Gregorio Marañón, *El Conde-Duque de Olivares: La pasión de mandar* (Madrid, 1936; 3rd, revised edn, 1952).
3. See the article on Hume in the *Oxford Dictionary of National Biography*, ed. H. C. G. Matthew and Brian Harrison, 60 vols (Oxford, 2004).
4. Martin Hume, 'La política centralizadora del Conde-Duque', *La Lectura*, 7 (1907), pp. 209–23.
5. I would later publish this document in full, under the title of the 'Gran Memorial', in John H. Elliott and José F. de la Peña (eds), *Memoriales y cartas del Conde Duque de Olivares*, 2 vols (Madrid, 1978–81), 1, doc. 4.
6. Fernand Braudel to the author, 10 December 1952.
7. A recent study by Michael Bentley of Butterfield as a historian, *The Life and Thought of Herbert Butterfield: History, Science and God* (Cambridge, 2011), fails, in my view, to convey an adequate impression of Butterfield as a research supervisor.

8. For further discussion of nationalist history, see below, ch. 2.

9. See the biography by Manuel Moreno Alonso, *El mundo de un historiador: Antonio Domínguez Ortiz* (Seville, 2009).

10. Later published under the title of *Dietari de Jeroni Pujades*, ed. J. M. Casas Homs, 4 vols (Barcelona, 1975–6). See also James Amelang, 'The Mental World of Jeroni Pujades', in Richard L. Kagan and Geoffrey Parker (eds), *Spain, Europe and the Atlantic World: Essays in Honour of John H. Elliott* (Cambridge, 1995), pp. 211–26.

11. Cristòfol Despuig, *Los col.loquis de la insigne ciutat de Tortosa* (1557), cited in J. H. Elliott, *The Revolt of the Catalans: A Study in the Decline of Spain, 1598–1640* (Cambridge, 1963), p. 13.

12. J. H. Elliott, *Imperial Spain, 1469–1716* (London, 1963).

13. See Elliott, *The Revolt of the Catalans*, pp. 30–2.

14. Clifford Geertz, *Local Knowledge: Further Essays in Interpretive Anthropology* (New York, 1983), pp. 55–6.

15. Ibid., pp. 56 and 58.

16. See Richard J. Evans, *Cosmopolitan Islanders: British Historians and the European Continent* (Cambridge, 2009).

17. For the fate of Robertson's *History* in Spain, see Jorge Cañizares-Esguerra, *How to Write the History of the New World* (Stanford, Calif., 2001), pp. 171–82.

18. The Black Legend has been the subject of many studies, beginning with the publication in 1914 of *La leyenda negra* by the Spaniard Julián Juderías, who invented the term. More recent accounts include Ricardo García Cárcel, *La leyenda negra: Historia y opinión* (Madrid, 1992), and Joseph Pérez, *La leyenda negra* (Madrid, 2009).

19. See below, ch. 4.

20. The word 'hispanista' is used in the title of an article by Miguel de Unamuno published in 1906, and '*hispanismo*' is defined in the *Diccionario de la literatura española* as 'the study of the language, literature and history of Spain by foreigners'. See Richard L. Kagan (ed.), *Spain in America: The Origins of Hispanism in the United States* (Urbana, Ill. and Chicago, 2002), pp. 2–3 and notes 3 and 4.

21. See below, p. 125.

22. Kenneth Clark, *Civilisation* (London, 1969), p. xvii.

2 National and transnational history

1. See above, p. 25.

2. Ferran Soldevila, *Història de Catalunya*, 3 vols (Barcelona, 1934–5). For Soldevila as a historian, see Enric Pujol, *Ferran Soldevila. Els fonaments de la historiografia contemporània* (Barcelona, 1995).

3. See Pujol, *Ferran Soldevila*, p. 37.

4. For Vicens's career, see Josep M. Muñoz i Lloret, *Jaume Vicens i Vives: Una biografia intel.lectual* (Barcelona, 1997).

5. J. H. Elliott, 'The Catalan Revolution of 1640: Some Suggestions for a Historical Revision', *Estudios de historia moderna*, 4 (1954), pp. 275–300.

6. Benedict Anderson, *Imagined Communities* (London and New York, 1983), p. 15.
7. See the examples in the set of conference papers edited by William R. Hutchinson and Hartmut Lehmann, *Many Are Chosen: Divine Election and Western Nationalism* (Harvard Theological Studies 38; Minneapolis, 1994).
8. See below, ch. 4.
9. *Times Literary Supplement*, 4 October 1963.
10. *History Today*, September 1963.
11. Juan Ramón Masoliver, *La Vanguardia Española*, 16 February 1967.
12. Francesco Espinet et al., 'L'historiador dalt del cavall: A propòsit de les reflexions d'un anglès sobre Catalunya i l'Europa del segle XVII', *El País-Quadern*, 277 (21 January 1988), pp. 1–3.
13. Pierre Vilar, *La Catalogne dans l'Espagne moderne*, 3 vols (Paris, 1962).
14. See Margaret MacMillan, *The Uses and Abuses of History* (London, 2009), pp. 86–8.
15. For the most recent attempt to redress the balance, see Daniel K. Richter, *Before the Revolution: America's Ancient Pasts* (Cambridge, Mass., and London, 2011), and my review 'The Very Violent Road to America', *New York Review of Books*, 9 June, 2011.
16. There are innumerable accounts of the emergence of modern nationalism. Among the most helpful, in addition to Benedict Anderson's *Imagined Communities*, are E. J. Hobsbawm, *Nations and Nationalism since 1780: Programme, Myth, Reality* (Cambridge, 1990), and Anthony D. Smith, *The Nation in History* (Hanover, NH, 2000).
17. Lucien Febvre, *Philippe II et la Franche-Comté* (Paris, 1912), pp. 43–4.
18. See Hobsbawm, *Nations and Nationalism*, pp. 54–7, 119–20.
19. See James S. Amelang, *Honored Citizens of Barcelona: Patrician Culture and Class Relations, 1490–1714* (Princeton, 1986), pp. 190–5.
20. See Joan-Lluís Marfany, *La llengua maltractada: El castellà i el català a Catalunya del segle XVI al segle XIX* (Barcelona, 2001).
21. See, for instance, 'King and *Patria* in the Hispanic World', in J. H. Elliott, *Spain, Europe and the Wider World, 1500–1800* (New Haven and London, 2009), ch. 9, and 'Revolution and Continuity in Early Modern Europe', *Past and Present*, 42 (1969), pp. 35–56, reprinted in J. H. Elliott, *Spain and its World, 1500–1700* (New Haven and London, 1989), ch. 5.
22. For the distinction between the language of patriotism and that of nationalism, see Maurizio Viroli, *For Love of Country: An Essay on Patriotism and Nationalism* (Oxford, 1996), although the book's primary concern is to trace the republican tradition of civic virtue.
23. J. G. A. Pocock, *The Ancient Constitution and the Feudal Law* (Cambridge, 1957).
24. Elliott, *The Revolt of the Catalans*, pp. 44–8.
25. See Elliott, *Spain and its World*, pp. 104–9.
26. The origins and development of the notion of a distinctive early modern period are currently the theme of a project being conducted in Saarland University by Professor Wolfgang Behringer and Dr Justus Nipperdey.

27. Sir Ernest Barker, Sir George Clark and P. Vaucher (eds) *The European Inheritance*, 3 vols (Oxford, 1954).

28. 'Most states in the early modern period were composite states.' See his 1975 inaugural lecture at King's College, London, '*Dominium politicum et regale*', reprinted in H. G. Koenigsberger, *Politicians and Virtuosi* (London, 1986), p. 12. See also my article 'A Europe of Composite Monarchies', *Past and Present*, 137 (1992), pp. 48–71, reprinted in Elliott, *Spain, Europe and the Wider World*, ch. 1.

29. For a survey of this debate, see my 'The General Crisis in Retrospect: A Debate without End', in Elliott, *Spain, Europe and the Wider World*, ch. 3. I originally published this piece, in a slightly different form, in a volume in honour of T. K. Rabb, one of the participants in the debate: Philip Benedict and Myron P. Gutmann (eds), *Early Modern Europe: From Crisis to Stability* (Newark, Del., 2005). The volume includes (pp. 25–30) a bibliographical listing of works relating to the seventeenth-century crisis. Since then, the *American Historical Review* has published a Forum on 'The General Crisis of the Seventeenth Century Revisited' (113, 2008, pp. 1029–99), while the Autumn 2009 issue of the *Journal of Interdisciplinary History* (11:2) is devoted to 'The Crisis of the Seventeenth Century: Interdisciplinary Perspectives'. The crisis in a global context is the subject of a forthcoming book by Geoffrey Parker, *Global Crisis* (New Haven and London, 2013).

30. H. R. Trevor-Roper, 'The General Crisis of the Seventeenth Century', *Past and Present*, 16 (1959), pp. 31–64, reprinted, along with other contributions to the debate, including my own, in Trevor Aston (ed.), *Crisis in Europe, 1550–1660* (London, 1965).

31. The renewed interest in the state and state-formation is exemplified by the multi-volume project sponsored by the European Science Foundation entitled 'The Origins of the Modern State in Europe, 13th–18th Centuries', under the general editorship of Wim Blockmans and Jean-Philippe Genet. See in particular the volume edited by Wolfgang Reinhard, *Power Elites and State Building* (Oxford, 1996).

32. See Felix Gilbert (ed.), *The Historical Essays of Otto Hintze* (New York, 1975), especially ch. 8 ('The Preconditions of Representative Government in the Context of World History'). The original German version was published in the *Historische Zeitschrift*, 143 (1931), pp. 1–47.

33. F. L. Carsten, *Princes and Parliaments in Germany from the Fifteenth to the Eighteenth Century* (Oxford, 1959); see also my review article 'Princes and Parliaments', *Past and Present*, 17 (1960), pp. 82–7.

34. Conrad Russell, *The Causes of the English Civil War* (Oxford, 1990), p. 29.

35. Inaugural lecture given at the Queen's University of Belfast on 21 January 1955, reprinted in Michael Roberts, *Essays in Swedish History* (London, 1967), ch. 7. This essay gave rise to a prolonged and continuing discussion, in which my former graduate student Geoffrey Parker has played an especially prominent part. See his *The Military Revolution* (Cambridge, 1988), and also the review article by David Parrott 'The Constraints on Power: Recent Works on Early Modern European History', *European History Quarterly*, 30 (1990), pp. 101–9.

36. James Casey, *The Kingdom of Valencia in the Seventeenth Century* (Cambridge, 1979), p. 201. See also my 'A Non-Revolutionary Society: Castile in the 1640s', in *Spain, Europe and the Wider World*, ch. 4, which addresses the same problem.
37. For a good example, see Sharon Kettering, *Patrons, Brokers, and Clients in Seventeenth-Century France* (Oxford, 1986).
38. See William Beik, *Absolutism and Society in Seventeenth-Century France: State Power and Provincial Aristocracy in Languedoc* (Cambridge, 1985).
39. Sir George Clark, *War and Society in the Seventeenth Century* (Cambridge, 1958).
40. See Theodore K. Rabb, *The Struggle for Stability in Early Modern Europe* (New York, 1975), and, for England, J. H. Plumb, *The Growth of Political Stability in England, 1675–1725* (London, 1967).
41. J. H. Elliott, *Europe Divided, 1559–1598* (London, 1968; 2nd, revised edn, Oxford, 2000). The series, originally known as the Fontana History of Europe, and subsequently reissued under the title of Blackwell Classic Histories of Europe, was under the general editorship of J. H. Plumb.
42. Clark, *War and Society*, p. 26.
43. See my essay 'Learning from the Enemy: Early Modern Britain and Spain', in Elliott, *Spain, Europe and the Wider World*, ch. 2.
44. For a set of essays on the contrasting patterns, see Jon Arrieta and John H. Elliott (eds), *Forms of Union: The British and Spanish Monarchies in the Seventeenth and Eighteenth Centuries*, in *Riev* (*Revista internacional de los estudios vascos)*, Cuadernos 5 (Donostia, 2009).
45. See Louis Eisenmann, *Le compromis austro-hongrois de 1867* (Paris, 1904); see also, more recently, R. J. W. Evans, *Austria, Hungary, and the Habsburgs: Central Europe c. 1683–1867* (Oxford, 2006).
46. See the comparison of English and French financial arrangements in Roland Mousnier, 'L'évolution des finances publiques en France et en Angleterre pendant les guerres de la ligue d'Augsburg et de la succession d'Espagne', *Revue historique*, 205 (1951), pp. 1–23.
47. See Dietrich Gerhard, *Old Europe: A Study of Continuity, 1000–1800* (New York and London, 1981), which, while strong on the continuity, underplays the changes.
48. See Arno J. Mayer, *The Persistence of the Old Regime: Europe to the Great War* (New York, 1981).
49. See below, ch. 7.
50. The supranational theme of European unity emerged strongly in the conferences and exhibitions, notably those held in Spain and Belgium, that celebrated the quincentenary in 2000 of the birth of Charles V.
51. See Norman Davies, *The Isles: A History* (London, 1999).

3 Political history and biography

1. See above, p. 16.
2. D. L. M. Avenel (ed.), *Lettres, instructions diplomatiques et papiers d'état du cardinal de Richelieu*, 8 vols (Paris, 1853–77); Gabriel Hanotaux and the

Duc de La Force, *Histoire du cardinal de Richelieu*, 6 vols (Paris, 1893–1947).

3. See above, pp. 7–8.

4. Antonio Cánovas del Castillo, *Estudios del reinado de Felipe IV*, 2 vols (Madrid, 1888).

5. Elliott and la Peña (eds), *Memoriales y cartas*. Tragically, José Francisco de la Peña died in 1994 at the age of fifty. I am currently planning with Spanish colleagues a third volume, containing the important correspondence between the Count-Duke and Philip IV's brother the Cardinal-Infante during the period of his government of Flanders.

6. See, however, Lucien Febvre, *Un destin: Martin Luther* (Paris, 1928), which he describes in his foreword as neither a biography nor a 'judgment', but an attempt 'to pose, in relation to a man of singular vitality, the problem of the relationship of the individual to the collectivity, of personal initiative to social necessity, which is, perhaps, the capital problem of history'.

7. Fernand Braudel, *The Mediterranean and the Mediterranean World in the Age of Philip II*, trans. Siân Reynolds, 2 vols (London, 1972–3), 2, p. 1244.

8. In addition to the comments made by Peter Burke, *The French Historical Revolution: The Annales School, 1929–1989* (Cambridge, 1990), pp. 40–1, on the charge of determinism levelled against Braudel by his critics, including myself, see the pointed observations on Braudel's view of the biographical approach to history made by Derek Beales in the inaugural lecture 'History and Biography' delivered in Cambridge in 1981. The lecture was reprinted in T. C. W. Blanning and David Cannadine (eds), *History and Biography: Essays in Honour of Derek Beales* (Cambridge, 1996), where the observations can be found on pp. 268–70.

9. Fernand Braudel, 'En Espagne au temps de Richelieu et d'Olivares', *Annales: ESC*, 2 (1947), pp. 354–8.

10. See Pedro Laín Entralgo, *Gregorio Marañón: Vida, obra y persona* (Madrid, 1969), pp. 97–8.

11. For Spanish psychiatry in this period, see Michael Richards, 'Spanish Psychiatry c.1900–1945: Constitutional Theory, Eugenics, and the Nation', *Bulletin of Spanish Studies*, 81 (2004), pp. 823–48. I am indebted to Dr James Amelang for this reference.

12. Gregorio Marañón, *El Conde-Duque de Olivares: La pasión de mandar* (Madrid, 1936; 3rd, revised edn, 1952), pp. 4–5.

13. Ibid., p. 63.

14. For the turn of the *Annales* school to the history of *mentalités*, see Burke, *The French Historical Revolution*, ch. 4 ('The Third Generation'). It is important to recognize, however, as Burke makes clear, that there had always been historians in the *Annales* group with a strong interest in cultural history.

15. Braudel, *The Mediterranean*, 1, p. 21.

16. Antonio Domínguez Ortiz, *Política y hacienda de Felipe IV* (Madrid, 1960); see also above, p. 22.

17. Antonio Domínguez Ortiz, *La sociedad española en el siglo XVII*, 2 vols (Madrid, 1963–70).

18. José Antonio Maravall, *La cultura del barroco* (Barcelona, 1975); English translation by Terry Cochran, *Culture of the Baroque: Analysis of a Historical Structure* (Minneapolis, 1986). See also my review 'Concerto Barroco', *New York Review of Books*, 9 April 1987.

19. See Michael Bentley, *The Life and Thought of Herbert Butterfield* (Cambridge, 2011), pp. 321–3.

20. J. H. Elliott, *Richelieu and Olivares* (Cambridge, 1984); see also below, ch. 6.

21. Jonathan Brown and John H. Elliott, *A Palace for a King: The Buen Retiro and the Court of Philip IV* (New Haven and London, 1980; revised and expanded edition, 2003); see also below, ch. 5.

22. A point made by Raymond Carr in his review 'The Don Quixote of Diplomacy', *New York Review of Books*, 20 November 1986.

23. Ronald Syme, *The Roman Revolution* (Oxford, 1939), p. 7.

24. Lewis Namier, *The Structure of Politics at the Accession of George III* (London, 1929), and *England in the Age of the American Revolution* (London, 1963); see also Linda Colley, *Lewis Namier* (London, 1989).

25. See Keith Thomas, *Changing Conceptions of National Biography* (Cambridge, 2005), p. 51.

26. For a number of examples, see the essays in Anthony Pagden (ed.), *The Languages of Political Theory in Early-Modern Europe* (Cambridge, 1987).

27. See John H. Elliott, *El Conde-Duque de Olivares y la herencia de Felipe II* (Valladolid, 1977), and 'A Question of Reputation? Spanish Foreign Policy in the Seventeenth Century', *Journal of Modern History*, 55 (1983), pp. 474–83, a review article which ends by asking for a prosopographical approach to the men of Spain's last great imperial generation.

28. For the possibilities, and the traps, presented by the study of key words, see especially Quentin Skinner, *Visions of Politics*, 3 vols (Cambridge, 2002), 1, ch. 9 ('The Idea of a Cultural Lexicon').

29. See, for instance, Roger Chartier, *L'ordre des livres: Lecteurs, auteurs, bibliothèques en Europe entre XIVe et XVIIIe siècles* (Aix-en-Provence, 1992); English translation by Lydia G. Cochrane, *The Order of Books: Readers, Authors, and Libraries in Europe between the Fourteenth and Eighteenth Centuries* (Cambridge, 1994). For a splendid study of the personal library of Philip IV of Spain, see Fernando Bouza, *El libro y el cetro: La biblioteca de Filipe IV en la Torre Alta del Alcázar de Madrid* (Madrid, 2005).

30. A major project, under the auspices of the Department of Spanish, Portuguese and Latin American Studies of the University of Nottingham, is currently under way for a study of the Count-Duke's library. The proceedings of a conference held in relation to this project have been published under the title *Poder y saber: Bibliotecas y bibliofilia en la época del conde-duque de Olivares*, ed. O. Noble Wood, J. Roe and J. Lawrance (Madrid, 2011).

31. See Gerhard Oestreich, *Neostoicism and the Early Modern State* (Cambridge, 1982).

32. See Elliott, *The Revolt of the Catalans*, p. 41.

33. Ernst Kantorowicz, *The King's Two Bodies: A Study in Mediaeval Political Theology* (Princeton, 1957).

34. Clifford Geertz, *Negara: The Theater-State in Nineteenth-Century Bali* (Princeton, 1980).
35. See, for example, the essays in David Cannadine and Simon Price (eds), *Rituals of Royalty: Power and Ceremonial in Traditional Societies* (Cambridge, 1987); and below, ch. 5, for the court and court culture.
36. The changing character of the relationship between kingship and religion over the long seventeenth century has been usefully surveyed by Paul Kléber Monod, *The Power of Kings: Monarchy and Religion in Europe, 1589–1715* (New Haven and London, 1999).
37. Francisco Tomás Valiente, *Los validos en la monarquía española del siglo XVII* (Madrid, 1963; 2nd edn, Madrid, 1990).
38. Jean Bérenger, 'Pour une enquête européenne: Le problème du ministériat au XVIIe siècle', *Annales*, 29 (1974), pp. 166–92.
39. J. H. Elliott and L. W. B. Brockliss (eds), *The World of the Favourite* (New Haven and London, 1999).
40. J. H. Elliott, *The Count-Duke of Olivares: The Statesman in an Age of Decline* (New Haven and London, 1986).
41. *Diccionario biográfico español* (Madrid, 2011–12).

4 Perceptions of decline

1. Anthony Sampson, *The New Anatomy of Britain* (London, 1971), p. v. The citation comes from p. 382 of the Penguin edition of *Imperial Spain* (London, 2002).
2. See Martin Wiener, *English Culture and the Decline of the Industrial Spirit, 1850–1980* (Cambridge, 1981), pp. 160–2.
3. Peter Jenkins, 'Patient Britain', *New Republic*, 23 December 1985, p. 15. The author subsequently used them again in his book *Mrs. Thatcher's Revolution: The Ending of the Socialist Era* (Cambridge, Mass., 1988), p. 47.
4. Paul Kennedy (ed.), *Grand Strategies in War and Peace* (New Haven and London, 1991).
5. Jenkins, *Mrs. Thatcher's Revolution*, pp. 44 and 47.
6. Earl J. Hamilton, 'The Decline of Spain', *Economic History Review*, 1st series, 8 (1938), pp. 168–79, and *American Treasure and the Price Revolution in Spain, 1501–1650* (Cambridge, Mass., 1934).
7. J. H. Elliott, 'The Decline of Spain', *Past and Present*, 20 (1961), pp. 52–75, reprinted in Elliott, *Spain and its World*, ch. 10
8. See Christopher Clark, 'Power', in Ulinka Rublack (ed.), *A Concise Companion to History* (Oxford, 2011), ch. 6.
9. The intellectual lineage of *The Decline and Fall* has been most recently traced by J. G. A. Pocock in vol. 3 of his monumental study *Barbarism and Religion* (Cambridge, 2003). See also G. W. Bowersock, John Clive and Stephen Graubard (eds), *Edward Gibbon and the Decline and Fall of the Roman Empire*, originally published in *Daedalus*, 105:3 (1977), and Santo Mazzarino, *La fine del mondo antico* (Milan, 1959); English translation by George Holmes, *The End of the Ancient World* (London, 1966).

10. Roger B. Merriman, *The Rise of the Spanish Empire in the Old World and the New*, 4 vols (New York, 1918–34; repr., 1962).
11. Ibid., 4, pp. 680 and 671.
12. See Randolph Starn, 'Meaning-Levels in the Theme of Historical Decline', *History and Theory*, 14 (1975), pp. 1–31, and Peter Burke, 'Tradition and Experience: The Idea of Decline from Bruni to Gibbon', in Bowersock, Clive and Graubard (eds), *Edward Gibbon and the Decline and Fall*, pp. 137–52.
13. Ibn Khaldûn, *The Muqaddimah*, trans. Franz Rosenthal, 3 vols (2nd edn, Princeton, 1967).
14. See J. B. Bury, *The Idea of Progress* (London, 1920; repr., New York, 1955).
15. See K. W. Swart, *The Sense of Decadence in Nineteenth-Century France* (The Hague, 1964), pp.161–9.
16. Oswald Spengler, *The Decline of the West*, trans. Charles Francis Atkinson, 2 vols (London, 1926–8).
17. J. Huizinga, *The Waning of the Middle Ages* (London, 1955), p. 334.
18. Arnold Toynbee, *A Study of History*, abridged by D. C. Somervell (London, 1946). A second volume, covering Toynbee's later volumes, was published in 1957.
19. My own reaction may well have been shaped by the broadcast debate between Toynbee and Pieter Geyl in 1948, the year I discovered *A Study of History*. For Geyl's onslaughts on Toynbee, see Pieter Geyl, *Debates with Historians* (London, 1962), chs 5–8.
20. David C. McClelland, *The Achieving Society* (New York and London, 1961).
21. Carlo M. Cipolla, *The Economic Decline of Empires* (London, 1970); Jaime Vicens Vives, *An Economic History of Spain*, trans. Frances M. López-Morillas (Princeton, 1969).
22. For a brief survey of foreign observations before 1700, see J. N. Hillgarth, *The Mirror of Spain, 1500–1700* (Ann Arbor, 2000), ch. 14 ('The Celebration of Spanish Decline').
23. Cited in Elliott, *Spain, Europe and the Wider World*, p. 41.
24. 'Espagne', in the *Encyclopédie méthodique ou pour ordre de matières*, series 'Géographie moderne', 1 (Paris, 1783), pp. 554–68.
25. For the debate over Masson, see Richard Herr, *The Eighteenth-Century Revolution in Spain* (Princeton, 1958), pp. 220–30. See also Ricardo García Cárcel, *La leyenda negra: Historia y opinión* (Madrid, 1998), ch. 2, for eighteenth-century Spanish reactions to the Enlightenment in general and to Masson in particular.
26. For 'the generation of 1898', see the useful survey by H. Ramsden, *The 1898 Movement in Spain* (Manchester, 1974).
27. See Joseph Pérez, *La leyenda negra* (Madrid, 2009), p. 163; and for Costa and his unsuccessful efforts to promote reform, see Raymond Carr, *Spain, 1808–1939* (Oxford, 1966), pp. 525–8.
28. See Jenkins, *Mrs. Thatcher's Revolution*, pp. 35–6, citing E. J. Hobsbawm, *Industry and Empire* (London, 1968), p. 149.
29. See Swart, *The Sense of Decadence*, ch. 5 ('The Year of Disaster').

30. Cited in Pérez, *La leyenda negra* p. 241, n. 262.
31. Américo Castro, *La realidad histórica de España* (Mexico City, 1954), translated by Edmund King as *The Structure of Spanish History* (Princeton, 1954); Claudio Sánchez Albornoz, *España: Un enigma histórico*, 2 vols (Buenos Aires, 1956; revised edn, 1962). For trenchant and entertaining comments on the controversy, see Peter Russell's review of Sánchez Albornoz, 'The Shirt of Nessus', *Bulletin of Hispanic Studies*, 36 (1959), pp. 219–25.
32. Jaime Vicens Vives, *Approaches to the History of Spain*, trans. and ed. Joan Connelly Ullman (Berkeley and Los Angeles, 1967), p. xxii.
33. He had previously looked at the work of some of them in 'Spanish Mercantilism before 1700', an essay published in *Facts and Factors in Economic History* (Cambridge, Mass., 1932), pp. 214–39.
34. Pierre Vilar, 'Le temps du Quichotte', *Europe*, 34 (1956), pp. 3–16; English translation, 'The Age of Don Quixote', in Peter Earle (ed.), *Essays in European Economic History, 1500–1800* (Oxford, 1974), pp. 100–13.
35. See David A. Lupher, *Romans in a New World: Classical Models in Sixteenth-Century Spanish America* (Ann Arbor, 2003).
36. For Sallust and Orosius, see Mazzarino, *The End of the Ancient World*, pp. 27–8, 58–61, and Pocock, *Barbarism and Religion*, 3, pp. 35–7, 78–86.
37. J. H. Elliott, 'Self-Perception and Decline in Seventeenth-Century Spain', *Past and Present*, 74 (1977), pp. 52–75, reprinted in Elliott, *Spain and its World*, ch. 11.
38. See Elliott and la Peña (eds), *Memoriales y cartas*, 2, p. 176.
39. See Jenkins, *Mrs. Thatcher's Revolution*, p. 42.
40. Paul Kennedy, *The Rise and Fall of the Great Powers* (New York, 1987), p. 515.
41. See Henry Kamen, 'The Decline of Spain: A historical myth?', *Past and Present*, 81 (1978), pp. 24–50, and the response by Jonathan Israel, *Past and Present*, 91 (1981), pp. 170–80.
42. For a recent bold but imperfect attempt to determine the course of Spain's economic trajectory over some four centuries, see Carlos Álvarez-Nogal and Leandro Prados de la Escosura, 'The Decline of Spain (1500–1850): Conjectural estimates', *European Review of Economic History*, 11 (2007), pp. 319–66. The authors suggest (pp. 321–2) that under Charles V and Philip II 'Spanish per capita income was among the highest in Europe, second only to Italy and the Low Countries. Since the 1590's Spain experienced an absolute decline that only became relative in the early nineteenth century.'
43. See below, ch. 7.
44. For a reassessment along these lines by a British historian, see Christopher Storrs, *The Resilience of the Spanish Monarchy, 1665–1700* (Oxford, 2006), which, however, is careful not to push the argument too far.
45. Cited in A. D. Momigliano, 'Gibbon's Contribution to Historical Method', in *Studies in Historiography* (New York and Evanston, Ill. 1966), p. 49 (the essay was originally published in *Historia*, 2, 1954).

5 Art and cultural history

1. Jonathan Brown and John H. Elliott. *A Palace for a King. The Buen Retiro and the Court of Philip IV* (New Haven and London, 1980; revised and expanded edition, 2003).

2. Millard Meiss, *Painting in Florence and Siena after the Black Death: The Arts, Religion, and Society in the Mid-Fourteenth Century* (Princeton, 1961).

3. Jonathan Brown, *Images and Ideas in Seventeenth-Century Spanish Painting* (Princeton, 1978), p. 15.

4. Per Palme, *Triumph of Peace: A Study of the Whitehall Banqueting House* (Stockholm, 1956).

5. George Kubler, *Building the Escorial* (Princeton, 1982). A later, more comprehensive and less idiosyncratic account is provided by Agustín Bustamante García, *Octava maravilla del mundo: Estudio histórico sobre el Escorial de Felipe II* (Madrid, 1994).

6. See Arnold Hauser, *Mannerism: The Crisis of the Renaissance and the Origins of Modern Art*, 2 vols (London, 1965).

7. Cited in Francis Haskell, *History and its Images: Art and the Interpretation of the Past* (New Haven and London, 1993), p. 490.

8. See Haskell, *History and its Images*, especially pp. 363 and 489–90.

9. See the catalogue to an exhibition of landscape painting in early seventeenth-century Rome, held first in the Louvre and then in the Prado: *Roma: Naturaleza e ideal: Paisajes 1600–1650* (Madrid, 2011).

10. For later reflections on the series and its significance, see the essay by Giovanna Capitelli, 'The Landscapes for the Buen Retiro Palace', written for the catalogue of an exhibition held in the Prado Museum in 2005 of works commissioned or acquired for the Buen Retiro: Andrés Úbeda de los Cobos (ed.), *Paintings for the Planet King: Philip IV and the Buen Retiro Palace* (Madrid and London, 2005), pp. 241–61; see also Úbeda de los Cobos, 'Las pinturas de paisaje para el palacio del Buen Retiro de Madrid', in *Roma: Naturaleza e ideal*, pp. 69–77.

11. Francis Haskell, *Patrons and Painters: Art and Society in Baroque Italy* (London, 1963; repr., Icon edn, New York, 1971).

12. Ibid., p. xviii.

13. Michael Baxandall, *Painting and Experience in Fifteenth-Century Italy* (Oxford, 1972), p. 3.

14. For imagery and responses to it, see David Freedberg, *The Power of Images* (Chicago, 1989).

15. José Antonio Maravall, *Culture of the Baroque: Analysis of a Historical Structure*, trans. Terry Cochran (Minneapolis, 1986), p. 72.

16. Norbert Elias, *The Court Society*, trans. Edmund Jephcott (Oxford and New York, 1983). This English edition did not appear until after Elias's *The Civilizing Process*, 2 vols (Oxford, 1978–82). For a discussion of Elias and his work, see Jeroen Duindam, *Myths of Power* (Amsterdam, 1995).

17. For a careful discussion of the various arguments, see Duindam, *Myths of Power*.

18. A. G. Dickens (ed.), *The Courts of Europe: Politics, Patronage and Royalty, 1400–1800* (London, 1977). A more recent survey of early modern courts indicates how court studies have moved on since the 1970s. Not only is Elias's model of absolutism specifically rejected, but a new emphasis is now being placed on the religious aspects of court life and ritual, and on the language of gesture. See John Adamson (ed.), *The Princely Courts of Europe: Ritual, Culture and Politics under the Ancien Régime, 1500–1750* (London, 1999), especially the editor's introduction.

19. Frances A. Yates, *The Valois Tapestries* (London, 1959). See also, as further examples of her approach, the essays on the images and symbolism of monarchy in her *Astraea: The Imperial Theme in the Sixteenth Century* (London, 1975).

20. See, for example, Roy Strong, *Splendour at Court: Renaissance Spectacle and Illusion* (London, 1973), for a vivid exposition of these themes.

21. See especially Michael Levey, *Painting at Court* (London, 1973).

22. See Jonathan Brown, *Collected Writings on Velázquez* (New Haven and London, 2008), pp. 103–17 ('Enemies of Flattery: Velázquez's Portraits of Philip IV').

23. See Jonathan Brown and John Elliott (eds), *The Sale of the Century: Artistic Relations between Spain and Great Britain, 1604–1655* (New Haven and London, 2002).

24. For another example, see the catalogue of the exhibition of the baroque as an international style held at the Victoria and Albert Museum in 2009: Michael Snodin and Nigel Llewellyn (eds), *Baroque, 1620–1800: Style in the Age of Magnificence* (New Haven and London, 2009).

25. For an indication and examples of this new interest, see the *Journal of the History of Collections*, founded in 1989.

26. See Brown and Elliott, *A Palace for a King*, pp. 105 and 108. See also Jonathan Brown, *Kings and Connoisseurs* (New Haven and London, 1995), especially pp. 228–9.

27. Marcel Mauss, 'Essai sur le don: Forme et raison de l'échange dans les sociétés archaïques', *L'année sociologique*, n.s. 1 (1923–4), pp. 30–186; English translation by W. D. Halls, *The Gift: The Form and Reason for Exchange in Archaic Societies* (London, 1990).

28. See the introduction to Natalie Zemon Davis, *The Gift in Sixteenth-Century France* (Oxford, 2000), for Mauss and his influence.

29. For a collection of essays which display the recent growth of interest in this topic, see Elizabeth Cropper (ed.), *The Diplomacy of Art: Artistic Creation and Politics in Seicento Italy* (Villa Spelman Colloquia 7; Milan, 2000).

30. See Brown and Elliott, *A Palace for a King*, ch. 6. Also Elliott, *Spain and its World*, ch. 8 ('Power and Propaganda in the Spain of Philip IV').

31. See Palme, *Triumph of Peace*, and Ronald Forsyth Millen and Robert Erich Wolf, *Heroic Deeds and Mystic Figures: A New Reading of Rubens' Life of Maria de' Medici* (Princeton, 1989).

32. See John Rupert Martin, *The Decorations for the Pompa Introitus Ferdinandi* (London and New York, 1972).

33. For 'sites of political contestation', see Teofilo F. Ruiz, *A King Travels: Festive Traditions in Late Medieval and Early Modern Spain* (Princeton and Oxford, 2012), p. 9 and passim.
34. Carlo Ginzburg, *The Cheese and the Worms: The Cosmos of a Sixteenth-Century Miller*, trans. John and Anne Tedeschi (Baltimore and London, 1980). For another illuminating example of microhistory based on inquisition records, see Richard L. Kagan, *Lucrecia's Dreams: Politics and Prophecy in Sixteenth-Century Spain* (Berkeley, Los Angeles and Oxford, 1990).
35. See Maxine Berg, *A Woman in History: Eileen Power, 1889–1940* (Cambridge, 1996), pp. 113–35.
36. Judith C. Brown, *Immodest Acts: The Life of a Lesbian Nun in Renaissance Italy* (Oxford, 1986).
37. For a convenient sample of work on witchcraft, see Jonathan Barry, Marianne Hester and Gareth Roberts (eds), *Witchcraft in Early Modern Europe: Studies in Culture and Belief* (Cambridge, 1996).
38. Two major pioneering studies stand out: Keith Thomas, *Religion and the Decline of Magic* (London, 1971), and Stuart Clark, *Thinking with Demons: The Idea of Witchcraft in Early Modern Europe* (Oxford, 1997).
39. For a helpful discussion of this and other questions about the possibilities and limitations of the history of popular culture, see Peter Burke, *Popular Culture in Early Modern Europe* (London, 1978). For the world of carnival, see his ch. 7.
40. See Brown and Elliott, *A Palace for a King*, pp. 156–63.
41. See *El palacio del Buen Retiro y el nuevo museo del Prado* (Madrid, 2000), with a foreword by the then minister of culture, Mariano Rajoy. As the plans in this booklet make clear, there would also be sufficient space elsewhere in the building to display the series of Roman and landscape paintings commissioned or acquired for the palace, many of which are not currently on show.
42. Úbeda de los Cobos (ed.), *Paintings for the Planet King*.

6 Comparative history

1. Marc Bloch, 'Pour une histoire comparée des sociétés européennes', *Revue de synthèse historique*, 46 (1928), pp. 15–50.
2. See Benjamin Z. Kedar, 'Outlines for Comparative History Proposed by Practicing Historians', in Benjamin Z. Kedar (ed.), *Explorations in Comparative History* (Jerusalem, 2009), pp. 1–28. In writing this chapter I have drawn on Kedar's essay, and also on my own previous observations on the subject in my Oxford University inaugural lecture, *National and Comparative History* (Oxford, 1991), and in a lecture entitled 'Comparative History' given at the International Historical Congress 'A Historia a Debate' held in Santiago de Compostela in July 1993, and subsequently published in Carlos Barros (ed.), *Historia a debate*, 3 vols (Santiago de Compostela, 1995), 3, pp. 9–19.
3. Cited by Felix Gilbert in his introduction to *The Historical Essays of Otto Hintze* (New York, 1975), p. 23. For Hintze, see above, p. 66, and Kedar, *Explorations in Comparative History*, pp. 10–11.

4. See Fritz Redlich, 'Toward Comparative Historiography', *Kyklos*, 11 (1958), pp. 362–89.

5. For instance, by the anthropologist Julian Pitt-Rivers, in such works as *The People of the Sierra* (London, 1954), and *The Fate of Shechem; or, the Politics of Sex: Essays in the Anthropology of the Mediterranean* (Cambridge, 1977).

6. Barrington Moore, Jr, *Social Origins of Dictatorship and Democracy: Lord and Peasant in the Making of the Modern World* (London, 1967).

7. See above, pp. 63–5.

8. See, for example, Perez Zagorin, *Rebels and Rulers, 1500–1660*, 2 vols (Cambridge, 1982).

9. S. N. Eisenstadt, *The Political Systems of Empires: The Rise and Fall of Historical Bureaucratic Societies* (New York, 1963); Charles Tilly, *European Revolutions, 1492–1992* (Oxford, 1993); Theda Skocpol, *States and Social Revolutions* (Cambridge, 1979).

10. Theda Skocpol and Margaret Somers, 'The Uses of Comparative History in Macrosocial Inquiry', *Comparative Studies in Society and History*, 22 (1980), pp. 174–97.

11. Kevin Sharpe, *The Personal Rule of Charles I* (New Haven and London, 1992), p. 123.

12. Bloch, 'Pour une histoire comparée', p. 15.

13. See William H. Sewell, Jr, 'Marc Bloch and the Logic of Comparative History', *History and Theory*, 6 (1967), pp. 208–18.

14. Bloch, 'Pour une histoire comparée', p. 30, n. 1.

15. Fernand Braudel, *L'identité de la France*, 2 vols (Paris, 1986); English translation by Siân Reynolds, *The Identity of France*, 2 vols (London, 1987–91), 1, p. 21.

16. Clifford Geertz, *Islam Observed: Religious Development in Morocco and Indonesia* (Chicago, 1971). See Skocpol and Somers, 'The Uses of Comparative History', pp. 178–9, for this example.

17. Brian Pullan, *Rich and Poor in Renaissance Venice* (Oxford, 1971), and 'Catholics and the Poor in Early Modern Europe', *Transactions of the Royal Historical Society*, 5th series, 26 (1976), pp. 15–34.

18. Paul Slack, *Policy and Poverty in Tudor England* (Oxford, 1988), pp. 8–14. I have taken this example from my 'Comparative History', in *Historia a debate*, cited above.

19. Elliott, *Richelieu and Olivares*.

20. Ibid., pp. 25–7.

21. Ibid., p. 79.

22. For a theoretical discussion of the nature and possibilities of *histoire croisée*, see Michael Werner and Bénédicte Zimmermann, 'Beyond Comparison: *Histoire Croisée* and the Challenge of Reflexivity', *History and Theory*, 45 (2006), pp. 30–50.

23. George M. Fredrickson, 'The Status of Comparative History', in his *The Comparative Imagination: On the History of Racism, Nationalism and Social Movements* (Berkeley, Los Angeles and London, 1997), p. 24.

24. Jürgen Kocka, 'Comparative History: Methodology and Ethos', in Kedar (ed.), *Explorations in Comparative History*, p. 33.

25. Frank Tannenbaum, *Slave and Citizen: The Negro in the Americas* (New York, 1946).
26. See in particular David Brion Davis, *The Problem of Slavery in Western Culture* (Ithaca, NY, 1966), and Herbert S. Klein, *Slavery in the Americas: A Comparative Study of Virginia and Cuba* (Chicago, 1967).
27. Ronald Syme, *Colonial Élites: Rome, Spain and the Americas* (Oxford, 1958). For Syme, see above, p. 00.
28. James Lang, *Conquest and Commerce: Spain and England in the Americas* (New York, 1975).
29. Louis Hartz, *The Founding of New Societies* (New York, 1964), p. 3.
30. J. H. Elliott, *Empires of the Atlantic World: Britain and Spain in America, 1492–1830* (New Haven and London, 2006).
31. David Hume, 'Of National Characters', in *Essays: Moral, Political and Literary* (Oxford, 1963), p. 210.
32. Trevor Burnard, 'Empire Matters? The Historiography of Imperialism in Early America, 1492–1830', *History of European Ideas*, 33 (2007), pp. 87–107.

7 The wider picture

1. J. H. Hexter, *On Historians: Reappraisals of Some of the Masters of Modern History* (Cambridge, Mass., 1979), ch. 5 ('The Historical Method of C. Hill'), p. 242.
2. Emmanuel Le Roy Ladurie, *Paris–Montpellier P.C.–P.S.U., 1945–1963* (Paris, 1982), pp. 207–8.
3. Letter of 4 May 1999.
4. Jean Bodin, *Method for the Easy Comprehension of History*, trans. Beatrice Reynolds (New York, 1945), p. 301.
5. Alfred W. Crosby, *Ecological Imperialism: The Biological Expansion of Europe, 900–1900* (Cambridge, 1986; Canto edn, 1994), p. 7.
6. See Bernard Bailyn, *Atlantic History: Concepts and Contours* (Cambridge, Mass., 2005), ch. 1, for the idea of Atlantic history and its origins. There is now a large literature on Atlantic history. See in particular Jack P. Greene and Philip Morgan (eds), *Atlantic History: A Critical Appraisal* (Oxford, 2009), and Nicholas Canny and Philip Morgan (eds), *The Oxford Handbook of the Atlantic World, 1450–1850* (Oxford, 2011).
7. J. H. Elliott, *The Old World and the New, 1492–1650* (Cambridge, 1970; revised Canto edn, 1992).
8. Antonello Gerbi, *La disputa del Nuovo mondo: Storia di una polemica, 1750–1900* (Milan and Naples, 1955); English translation of revised and enlarged edition by Jeremy Moyle, *The Dispute of the New World: The History of a Polemic, 1750–1900* (Pittsburgh, 1973).
9. Earl J. Hamilton, *American Treasure and the Price Revolution in Spain, 1501–1650* (Cambridge, Mass., 1934); Pierre and Huguette Chaunu, *Séville et l'Atlantique*, 8 vols (Paris, 1955–9).
10. David Armitage, 'Three Concepts of Atlantic History', in David Armitage and Michael J. Braddick (eds), *The British Atlantic World, 1500–1800* (Basingstoke, 2002; 2nd edn, 2009), p. 11.

11. Ian K. Steele, *The English Atlantic, 1675–1740* (New York and Oxford, 1986), pp. 14–15.
12. See José C. Moya, 'Modernization, Modernity and the Trans/formation of the Atlantic World in the Nineteenth Century', in Jorge Cañizares-Esguerra and Erik R. Seeman (eds), *The Atlantic in Global History, 1500–2000* (Upper Saddle River, NJ, 2006), pp. 179–97.
13. Silver production in Potosí is the subject of two books by one of my former graduate students, Peter Bakewell: *Miners of the Red Mountain: Indian Labor in Potosí, 1545–1650* (Albuquerque, 1984) and *Silver and Entrepreneurship in Seventeenth-Century Potosí: The Life and Times of Antonio López de Quiroga* (Albuquerque, 1988).
14. See, for instance, Alison Games, *The Web of Empire: English Cosmopolitanism in an Age of Expansion, 1560–1660* (Oxford, 2008), Linda Colley, *The Ordeal of Elizabeth Marsh: A Woman in World History* (London, 2007), and Emma Rothschild, *The Inner Life of Empires: An Eighteenth-Century History* (Princeton, 2011).
15. Geoffrey Blainey, *The Tyranny of Distance: How Distance Shaped Australia's History* (Melbourne, 1966).
16. Nicholas Canny (ed.), *Europeans on the Move: Studies on European Migration, 1500–1800* (Oxford, 1994).
17. The term 'vision of the vanquished' seems to have been coined by the distinguished Mexican ethnographer and historian Miguel León-Portilla, who used it as the title of his anthology of indigenous accounts of the Spanish conquest, *Visión de los vencidos: Relaciones indígenas de la conquista* (Mexico City, 1959). 'The people without history' are the subject of a work by the North American anthropologist Eric R. Wolf, *Europe and the People without History* (Berkeley, Los Angeles and London, 1982).
18. Richard White, *The Middle Ground: Indians, Empires, and Republics in the Great Lakes Region, 1650–1815* (Cambridge, 1991), p. x.
19. See John E. Wills, *1688: A Global History* (London, 2001).
20. See C. A. Bayly, *The Birth of the Modern World, 1780–1914* (Oxford, 2004), ch. 2, for an admirably lucid discussion of some of the issues involved.
21. Kenneth Pomeranz, *The Great Divergence: China, Europe, and the Making of the Modern World Economy* (Princeton, 2000).
22. The term 'industrious revolution' was given currency by Jan de Vries, *The Industrious Revolution: Consumer Behavior and the Household Economy, 1650 to the Present* (Cambridge, 2008). It was coined by Akira Hayami to contrast the labour-intensive path of industrial development of Japan with the capital-intensive industrialization of the west (de Vries, p. 9, n. 27).
23. See Patrick O'Brien, 'Historiographical Traditions and Modern Imperatives for the Restoration of Global History', the prolegomenon to the first issue of the *Journal of Global History*, 1 (2006), pp. 3–39.
24. S. N. Eisenstadt, 'The First Multiple Modernities: Collective Identities, Public Spheres and Political Order in the Americas', in Luis Roniger and Carlos H.

Waisman (eds), *Globality and Multiple Modernities* (Brighton, 2002), ch. 2; see also his 'Multiple Modernities', *Daedalus*, 129:1 (2000), pp. 1–29.

25. *The Complete Plays and Poems of T. S. Eliot* (London, 1969), p. 147 (Chorus 1 from *The Rock*).

26. Leopold Ranke, *The Ottoman and the Spanish Empires in the Sixteenth and Seventeenth Centuries*, trans. Walter B. Kelly (London, 1843).

Select bibliography

This bibliography is confined to those publications of the author to which reference is made in the text (listed here by date of publication). Full bibliographical details of works by other authors cited in the book are given at each first reference, and are repeated if they appear again in later chapters.

Books

The Revolt of the Catalans: A Study in the Decline of Spain, 1598–1640 (Cambridge, 1963)

Imperial Spain, 1469–1716 (London, 1963; revised repr., 2002)

Europe Divided, 1559–1598 (London, 1968; 2nd revised edn, Oxford, 2000)

The Old World and the New, 1492–1650 (Cambridge, 1970; revised edn, 1992)

John H. Elliott and José F. de la Peña (eds), *Memoriales y cartas del Conde Duque de Olivares*, 2 vols (Madrid, 1978–81)

Jonathan Brown and John H. Elliott, *A Palace for a King: The Buen Retiro and the Court of Philip IV* (New Haven and London, 1980; revised and expanded edn, 2003)

Richelieu and Olivares (Cambridge, 1984)

The Count-Duke of Olivares: The Statesman in an Age of Decline (New Haven and London, 1986)

Spain and its World, 1500–1700 (New Haven and London, 1989)

J. H. Elliott and L. W. B. Brockliss (eds), *The World of the Favourite* (New Haven and London, 1999)

Jonathan Brown and John Elliott (eds), *The Sale of the Century: Artistic Relations between Spain and Great Britain, 1604–1655* (New Haven and London, 2002)

Empires of the Atlantic World: Britain and Spain in America, 1492–1830 (New Haven and London, 2006)

Spain, Europe and the Wider World, 1500–1800 (New Haven and London, 2009)

Jon Arrieta and John H. Elliott (eds), *Forms of Union: The British and Spanish Monarchies in the Seventeenth and Eighteenth Centuries*, in *Riev (Revista internacional de los estudios vascos)*, Cuadernos 5 (Donostia, 2009)

Articles and lectures

'The Catalan Revolution of 1640: Some Suggestions for a Historical Revision', *Estudios de historia moderna*, 4 (1954), pp. 275–300

'Princes and Parliaments', *Past and Present*, 17 (1960), pp. 82–7

Contribution to discussion of H. R. Trevor–Roper's 'The General Crisis of the Seventeenth Century', *Past and Present*, 18 (1960), pp. 25–31, reprinted in Trevor Aston (ed.), *Crisis in Europe, 1560–1660* (London, 1965), ch. 4

'The Decline of Spain', *Past and Present*, 20 (1961), pp. 52–75, reprinted in *Spain and its World, 1500–1700*, ch. 10

'Revolution and Continuity in Early Modern Europe', *Past and Present*, 42 (1969), pp. 35–56 reprinted in *Spain and its World, 1500–1700*, ch. 5

'Self-Perception and Decline in Seventeenth-Century Spain', *Past and Present*, 74 (1977), pp. 52–75, reprinted in *Spain and its World, 1500–1700*, ch. 11

El Conde-Duque de Olivares y la herencia de Felipe II (Valladolid, 1977)

'A Question of Reputation? Spanish Foreign Policy in the Seventeenth Century', *Journal of Modern History*, 55 (1983), pp. 474–83

'A Non-Revolutionary Society: Castile in the 1640s', in *Études d'histoire européenne: Mélanges offerts à René et Suzanne Pillorget* (Angers, 1990), pp. 253–69, reprinted in *Spain, Europe and the Wider World, 1500–1800*, ch. 4

National and Comparative History: An Inaugural Lecture (Oxford, 1991)

'A Europe of Composite Monarchies', *Past and Present*, 137 (1992), pp. 48–71, reprinted in *Spain, Europe and the Wider World, 1500–1800*, ch. 1

'Comparative History', in Carlos Barros (ed.), *Historia a debate*, 3 vols (Santiago de Compostela, 1995), 3, pp. 9–19

'The General Crisis in Retrospect: A Debate without End', in *Spain, Europe and the Wider World, 1500–1800*, ch. 3

'Learning from the Enemy: Early Modern Britain and Spain', in *Spain, Europe and the Wider World, 1500–1800*, ch. 2

'King and *Patria* in the Hispanic World', in *Spain, Europe and the Wider World, 1500–1800*, ch. 9 (originally published in Spanish as 'Rey y patria en el mundo hispánico', in Victor Mínguez and Manuel Chust (eds), *El imperio sublevado* (Madrid, 2004), pp. 17–35

Book reviews

'Concerto Barroco', *New York Review of Books*, 9 April 1987

'The Very Violent Road to America', *New York Review of Books*, 9 June 2011

Index